MW00861655

TEACHING KIDS TO
PAUSE, COPE,

AND CONNECT

LESSONS FOR SOCIAL EMOTIONAL LEARNING AND MINDFULNESS

MARK PURCELL, PSY.D. • KELLEN GLINDER, M.D.

free spirit
PUBLISHING®

Copyright © 2022 by Mark Purcell and Kellen Glinder

All rights reserved under International and Pan-American Copyright Conventions. Unless otherwise noted, no part of this book may be reproduced, stored in a retrieval system, or transmitted in any form or by any means, electronic, mechanical, photocopying, recording, or otherwise, without express written permission of the publisher, except for brief quotations or critical reviews. For more information, go to freespirit.com/permissions.

Free Spirit, Free Spirit Publishing, and associated logos are trademarks and/or registered trademarks of Teacher Created Materials. A complete listing of our logos and trademarks is available at freespirit.com.

Library of Congress Cataloging-in-Publication Data
This book has been filed with the Library of Congress.
ISBN: 978-63198-347-4

Free Spirit Publishing does not have control over or assume responsibility for author or third-party websites and their content. At the time of this book's publication, all facts and figures cited within are the most current available. All telephone numbers, addresses, and website URLs are accurate and active; all publications, organizations, websites, and other resources exist as described in this book; and all have been verified as of January 2022. If you find an error or believe that a resource listed here is not as described, please contact Free Spirit Publishing.

Permission is granted to reproduce the pages included in the List of Reproducibles (page ix) or in the digital content that goes with this book for individual, classroom, and small group use only. Other photocopying or reproduction of these materials is strictly forbidden. For licensing and permissions information, contact the publisher.

Illustrations in book: © Libux77 | Dreamstime.com; © Olga Galeeva | Dreamstime.com; © Stas11 | Dreamstime.com; © Yanisa Deeratanasrikul | Dreamstime.com; © Spideyspike32 | Dreamstime.com; © Chatsuda Megmuangthong | Dreamstime.com; © Hanna Vauchkova | Dreamstime.com © Sommersby | Dreamstime.com; © Evgenii Naumov | Dreamstime.com; © Punnawich Limparungpatanakij | Dreamstime.com; © Irina Miroshnichenko | Dreamstime.com; © Microvone | Dreamstime.com; © Dariia Baranova | Dreamstime.com; © Patrick Marcel Pelz | Dreamstime.com; © Ssstocker | Dreamstime.com; © Lio Putra | Dreamstime.com; © Tina Nizova | Dreamstime.com; © Roman Egorov | Dreamstime.com; © Alhovik | Dreamstime.com; © Yusuf Demirci | Dreamstime.com

Edited by Margie Lisovskis, Ruthie Nelson Van Oosbree, and Christine Zuchora-Walske
Cover design by Shannon Pourciau; interior design by Shannon Pourciau and Michelle Lee Lagerroos

Printed in the United States of America

Free Spirit Publishing
An imprint of Teacher Created Materials
9850 51st Avenue, Suite 100
Minneapolis, MN 55442
(612) 338-2068
help4kids@freespirit.com
freespirit.com

Free Spirit offers competitive pricing.

Contact edsales@freespirit.com for pricing information on multiple quantity purchases.

Dedication

For Veronica, who is a perpetual champion for the social and emotional health of children, especially our own. —M. P.

For Judy, Sophie, and Beckett, who have shown me the power of being present. —K. G.

Acknowledgments

This project saw many forms before materializing as a book. It certainly took a village—and a community—to get here. We would like to thank the folks at Free Spirit Publishing who believed that this was a much-needed project. Along the way we found inspiration from the late monk Thich Nhat Hahn, who tirelessly advocated for the mindfulness and playful spirit of children throughout the world, as well as from our own walking meditations through the caverns of Kepler's Books, a mindful sanctuary in the heart of Silicon Valley. Thank you to Linda Creighton, principal of Laurel Elementary School, and Gatee Esmat, principal of Arroyo Seco Elementary, who invited us in and welcomed our efforts. Teachers Ms. Mazzoncini, Ms. Reagan, Ms. Scher, and Ms. Baker helped guide our early efforts, and Sarah Newman at themindfulkids.com kept us on the right path. Lastly, we would like to thank you for your interest in the mental health of our next generation. We can make no investment too large for their future, and staying attuned to the needs of our children is a great way to build the community they need.

CONTENTS

List of Figures

List of Reproducibles

ADDitional Material in Digital Format

Bonus Life Skill: Feel Safe

    Lesson: I Am Safe (Pause)

    Lesson: Stay Grounded (Cope)

    Lesson: Hawks and Lizards (Connect)

Bonus Life Skill: Seek Joy

    Lesson: Happy Place (Pause)

    Lesson: Play Hard (Cope)

    Lesson: Silly Skits (Connect)

Bonus Reproducibles

    Stay Grounded

    My Happy Place

    All the Things I Can Do

    Making Time for Fun

See page 186 for instructions on how to download the reproducible forms and other digital content for this book.

INTRODUCTION

Mindfulness is ultimately about empathy. Through pausing to listen intently to how we feel, what thoughts we have, and what others are telling us, we develop compassion for ourselves and others. This is a biochemical process: mindfulness has been found to reduce stress hormone levels, blood pressure, and heart rate. It also raises oxytocin, the hormone of compassion. The compassion built through mindfulness practice helps teach us empathy for each other and spread that empathy.

The ability to observe what we are feeling without reacting is a foundational aspect of mindfulness. In social-emotional learning (SEL), this skill is known as emotional regulation. You can teach mindfulness to your students and, in doing so, give them a skill that can support them throughout their lives at school and beyond. Once kids know how to stop, breathe, and observe their feelings and surroundings in lessons and practice sessions, they are ready to apply these skills to their own tumultuous emotional worlds. This book provides a series of lessons designed to introduce elementary school students to mindfulness practice and help them build social-emotional awareness.

When your students can calmly observe their own intense emotions without automatically reacting, they are ready to try mindful observation of their social situations. Some of the lesson plans in this book can help students navigate social situations mindfully and develop compassion and understanding for themselves and those around them. Cultivating that compassion will help you build a culture of empathy in your classroom.

Of course, it takes practice to build such a community. The lessons in this book can help make the practice easy to do within already-full classroom days. Simply repeating small mindfulness practices daily goes a long way in building the habits that contribute to an empathetic community.

Challenges for Today's Children

Children today face many challenges that did not exist a generation or two ago. Children and adolescents are experiencing stress at unprecedented levels. As a result, students are at increased risk for anger, anxiety, and depression, as well as lower self-esteem and self-confidence (Centers for Disease Control and Prevention 2021; Mendelson et al. 2010). Among five-to-fifteen-year-olds, rates of emotional disorders (including anxiety and depression) have increased steadily over the years, from 3.9 percent in 2004 to 5.8 percent in 2017 (CDC 2021). In addition, the COVID-19 pandemic that began in 2020 resulted in epidemic physical and mental health challenges for children. During the pandemic, rates of elevated depression and anxiety symptoms among children worldwide nearly doubled

pre-pandemic rates, from 12.9 percent to 25.2 percent for depression symptoms and from 11.6 percent to 20.5 percent for anxiety symptoms (Racine et al. 2021). Distance learning and social distancing led to increased isolation and social anxiety. More than ever, children need support to manage their emotions and form healthy connections.

Today's students also have more resources at their fingertips than any previous generation: smartphones, tablets, social media, and the internet. Yet as anyone who teaches or cares for children well knows, with all these technological resources, many students struggle with regulating their emotions, sustaining attention, and maintaining healthy social connections. The constant availability of electronic distractions creates an easy escape from difficult feelings and interactions and allows children to avoid uncomfortable situations. As they indulge in distractions and avoidance, challenging emotions fester and cause more stress—further preventing children from dealing with them. Elementary-age children who habitually rely on distractions during this critical period of early development can get really good at reflexively avoiding difficult emotions, and doing so often becomes so automatic that they never learn to confront these feelings. Daily, we see stressed-out, distracted children who struggle with simply tolerating uncomfortable feelings or direct social interactions.

As educators and parents, we often fall into similar patterns. When we see that a child is upset, we immediately jump to fix it. We want to help them avoid pain. But sometimes we prevent them from learning to live life fully and cope with its highs *and* lows. What frustrated teacher hasn't sent two students to the office because of a conflict rather than sit through the tedious task of having them talk it out? And what parent hasn't fixed a painful and embarrassing store meltdown over an item they've denied their child by succumbing and indulging the tantrum? Of course, children then learn to tantrum and get their way instead of learning to cope with disappointment and discomfort. Situations like these happen in many different contexts. These dynamics may prevent some children from learning to tolerate distress or work through disappointment and conflict. When this pattern is repeated over time, or reinforced in society, it can lead to more serious social-emotional issues, such as anxiety and depression, as well as risk for future substance abuse.

The physical consequences of this inability to cope with difficult emotions can also be serious. Biological stress responses are automatic reactions to fear, and they are healthy in small and infrequent doses. But when continued avoidance causes constant, pervasive stress, the body starts to break down. Chronic stress causes high blood pressure, faster heart rates, over- or undereating, sleeplessness, restlessness, and secondary emotions of anger, aggression, isolation, and loneliness. Of course, these symptoms don't appear all at once—chronic stress changes our minds and bodies slowly—and they aren't identical in everyone, so we may have difficulty seeing these signs right away. Solutions take time too. Mindfulness can be an important remedy because it involves approaching our experiences with curiosity and acceptance

A NOTE ABOUT LANGUAGE

Throughout this book, we use the term *parents* to mean a student's primary caregiver(s) or legal guardian(s), while realizing that many children have a single parent and/or may not use the term *parent*.

rather than turning away from them. But like any other skill, it takes consistent practice to combat the distracted avoidance many of us experience daily.

To prevent these physical consequences of avoidance, it's important to teach children that disappointment and discomfort are part of life. As with the weather, there are sunny days and stormy days. The way to heal from pain and discomfort is to learn how to acknowledge it and work through it. Mindfulness is the first step in this process.

Jon Kabat-Zinn, known as the founding father of mindfulness-based stress reduction, defines mindfulness as "paying attention in a particular way: on purpose, in the present moment, and non-judgmentally" ([1994] 2014). Another definition of mindfulness is simply "focused observation without judgment" (Bishop et al. 2004). Mindfulness expert Tara Brach describes mindfulness as recognizing what we are experiencing (on the inside) and sticking with it (2018). Taken together, these definitions of mindfulness mean developing self-awareness to (1) notice what you are experiencing *right now*, without judgment, and (2) *not* do something to fix it, avoid it, or make it go away.

This simple, unwavering awareness is the first step toward working through a difficult experience or unpleasant feeling. Too often we blame the outside world (people and circumstances) for our discomfort, or we seek something external to fix our tumultuous internal state. Mindfulness also paves the path for deeper social-emotional awareness.

In *Teaching Kids to Pause, Cope, and Connect*, you will find tools to help students develop this fundamental life skill of looking inward for the cause of and solutions for their own social-emotional challenges. Mindfulness and SEL are complementary approaches that increase self-awareness and social competence. As children develop the capacity to observe their own thoughts, emotions, and bodily experiences, they can develop the capacity to *respond* to situations rather than simply *react*. As self-acceptance grows, so does the capacity to accept others.

The Benefits of Mindfulness and Social-Emotional Learning

Integrating mindfulness-based programs with SEL in schools and other youth organizations has a broad range of positive outcomes. Mindfulness-based interventions have been shown to improve self-regulation, mood, and social-emotional development (Mendelson et al. 2010).

The Collaborative for Academic, Social, and Emotional Learning (CASEL) describes SEL as the process through which we all acquire and apply the skills necessary to "develop healthy identities, manage emotions and achieve personal and collective goals, feel and show empathy for others, establish and maintain supportive relationships, and make responsible and caring decisions."

Many of the concepts and approaches presented in this book parallel those taught as part of SEL. We highlight outcomes that both practices have in common: observing emotions in order to manage them better, fostering empathy, creating healthy relationships, and responding thoughtfully instead of impulsively.

Mindfulness research indicates improved social-emotional functioning with continued practice. This book provides the practice, and teachers can implement it by using brief, regular activities that are engaging for students and easy to implement. Numerous studies show improved focus and performance for students who practice mindfulness regularly (Chiesa and Serretti 2009; Jha, Krompinger, and Baime 2007). Other studies show that mindfulness improves emotional regulation (Roemer, Williston, and Rollins 2015), diminishes reactivity, and improves focus (Goldin and Gross 2010; Ortner, Kilner, and Zelazo 2007). Students participating in mindfulness programs have also been found to develop more compassion and empathy for others (Condon et al. 2013).

In various studies, a broad range of mindfulness interventions with children have demonstrated significant positive outcomes:

- School-based mindfulness intervention can reduce perceived stress and modulate activity in a brain region associated with responses to fear and stress (Bauer et al. 2020).

- Exercise-based mindfulness practices, such as yoga and tai chi, have demonstrated a reduction in stress levels and an increase in resilience to stressful events in school-age children (Mendelson et al. 2010).

- Body-oriented mindfulness practices, such as breath work, body scanning, and walking meditation, help children focus. This type of mindfulness also helps kids self-soothe, sleep better, and be less distractible (Napoli et al. 2005; Abrams 2008; Singh et al. 2007).

- Children with learning disabilities who practiced mindful meditation experienced decreased anxiety, increased social skills, and improved academic performance (Beauchemin et al. 2008).

- A child-friendly variation of the Mindfulness-Based Stress Reduction (MBSR) program—an evidence-based, eight-week mindfulness training program designed to assist people with stress, anxiety, depression, and pain—improved students' attention, self-regulation, social skills, and general well-being. Several studies support the use of mindfulness to address anxiety and depression (Baer 2014; Semple and Lee 2011).

- A separate child-specific program called Mindfulness-Based Cognitive Therapy for Children (MBCT-C) shows promise in treating childhood anxiety, enhancing emotional regulation, and developing social-emotional resiliency (Semple and Lee 2011; Baer 2014).

The large, and ever-growing, body of research in mindfulness interventions for children and adolescents shows that mindfulness improves student attention and self-esteem across a broad range of ages, learning styles, and behavioral challenges. What's more, mindfulness-based practices naturally appeal to children because they teach self-management and empower students to play a key role in their own growth and development (Semple, Reid, and Miller 2005). Teaching mindfulness to students creates the potential for greater self-awareness, improved impulse control, and decreased emotional reactivity to challenging events (Oberle et al. 2012; Thompson and Gauntlett-Gilbert 2008).

The Mind-Body Connection

Today, it is common knowledge that the mind and body are connected when it comes to health and well-being. This connection is especially important for children and adolescents in the process of growing and developing. The mind affects the body in a number of significant ways. For example, anxiety and stress cause increased muscle tension, blood pressure, and heart rate and increase risk of other physical issues, such as headaches, insomnia, and more. Chronic stress can also lead to lower levels of the neurotransmitters in the brain that stabilize mood and bring feelings of happiness and well-being, physically contributing to depression and anxiety. Remaining calm and content when possible is an important factor in keeping our bodies healthy.

Meanwhile, the body affects the mind. Physical health affects our mental and emotional well-being. Exercise has been shown to relieve stress and improve depression as effectively as some medications (Kvam et al. 2016; Netz 2017) and helps us better cope with stress and anxiety. Unhealthy habits also impact our mental health and emotional well-being. Poor sleep hygiene and nutrition contribute to depression and anxiety. The overuse of video games, cell phones, and social media have been linked to depression, anxiety, and aggression (Männikkö et al. 2020). Taking care of our bodies keeps our minds in balance.

Mindfulness provides one of the best methods for addressing this mind-body dynamic. Practices like body scans can effectively reduce insomnia. Many of the world's best athletes use mindfulness techniques to improve performance. Soldiers use similar breathing techniques to maintain mental and physical stability under stress.

In a true emergency, our bodies automatically tense up even *before* our brains recognize fear. It is not always true that fear generates the tension. Often, the body provides the first indicator that we are becoming upset before our mind recognizes the emotion. Certain mindfulness practices teach us to focus on how our bodies feel and identify early indicators of our own emotional escalations. In the same way, negative thoughts (such as "No one likes me!") can be so scary they can trigger a "fight, flight, or freeze" response in our bodies when we are not actually in any immediate danger.

Throughout *Teaching Kids to Pause, Cope, and Connect*, we weave the mind-body connection into our mindfulness lessons, and we provide strategies for using each of these two channels to regulate the other. A psychologist and a pediatrician, we've drawn on our expertise in our respective fields to create effective strategies for teaching mindfulness to kids for their improved health and well-being of body and mind. We've worked closely with teachers to hone these approaches for effective use in a classroom setting.

Creating a Culture of Mindfulness and Social-Emotional Awareness

We wrote this book with the ambitious goal of reaching beyond coping skills to plant the seeds for nurturing communities. The book is designed to be a comprehensive resource for teaching mindfulness and social-emotional awareness to elementary school children. We have tried to make our advice flexible so that you can teach lessons in whatever way

serves your group. You do not need to have any previous experience in mindfulness or SEL to teach these lessons effectively. However, knowledge of core aspects of these areas will support your teaching, so we've created lists of these aspects, along with tips to keep in mind while teaching the skills and implementing the curriculum. We recommend taking the time to review the following before teaching the lessons in your classroom.

Teaching Core Aspects of Mindfulness

Learning mindfulness is like learning to ride a bike. We learn it best by simply doing it. Just like riding a bike, mindfulness may feel awkward and frustrating at first. But with practice, mindfulness can become a skill you use with ease that brings you joy and satisfaction.

The lessons in this book dive into each of the following characteristics of mindfulness. Having an awareness of these characteristics and using the techniques described here to encourage mindful behaviors outside of planned activities can reinforce the lessons in the book.

CHARACTERISTICS OF MINDFULNESS

Present Moment Awareness: When conducting activities that focus on being aware in the present moment, bring attention to what students are experiencing *right now*. Most of the thoughts triggering difficult emotions relate to dwelling on a past hurt or regret or on a future fear. Prompt students with questions like: **What are you feeling right now in your body? What are you feeling right now in your heart (in your emotions)? What are you thinking right now?** This present-moment attention can help them focus on what *is* rather than on anxious what-ifs.

Curiosity: Mindfulness is very much about curiosity. But it is a curiosity that's focused inward, on the experiences of the heart, mind, and body. Encourage students to "play detective" with their own feelings and thoughts. Awareness and observation are key skills for developing mindfulness.

Describing Instead of Judging or Labeling: Judgments and labels tend to take us away from our direct experience. When we judge, we typically label each experience (or person) as good or bad. As often as possible, encourage students to use descriptive words rather than judgmental labels. (For example, judging/labeling might be "He's mean—I hate him." Describing instead might be "He did a mean thing, and I didn't like that.") This can help students develop a more flexible growth mindset about their experiences.

Acceptance: The term *acceptance*, from a mindfulness perspective, means accepting life on life's terms. It does not always mean loving it or even liking it. Sometimes we need to accept some tough realities in our lives. The opposite of acceptance, in this context, is avoidance. Avoidance can cause a great deal of suffering, from emotional struggles like anxiety and depression to social problems like conflict and isolation. To help students practice acceptance, encourage them to work through difficult feelings rather than avoid dealing with them. Encourage them to practice self-acceptance of who they are and what they are feeling. With this practice, students gradually learn to accept others too.

A Sense of Wonder: Mindfulness can instill a sense of wonder in children and adults. By discarding our habitual ways of dealing with the world, we open ourselves up to experiencing the world in a new, fresh way. Encourage students to be creative, think outside the box, and absorb new experiences with the wonder of a small child.

Genuine Connection and Understanding: The attitudes and habits developed through mindfulness practice begin to extend outward toward others. As a result, mindfulness ultimately leads to more authentic and empathic connections. Encourage students to genuinely share their feelings with each other and listen carefully to what their classmates express. As a result, students and teachers can build a classroom community that is more open, welcoming, and kind.

Teaching Core Aspects of Social-Emotional Awareness

Learning to understand our emotions and the social context that we live in is a fundamental part of child development. However, for a multitude of reasons, many children struggle with developing some of the critical skills related to social-emotional awareness. A growing body of research has demonstrated the need to integrate social-emotional learning into our educational system (Durlak et al. 2011).

CASEL divides SEL into five key components: self-awareness, self-management, social awareness, relationship skills, and responsible decision-making. The lessons in this book are designed to enhance students' understandings of these core areas. Structured activities provide opportunities to practice and begin mastering these essential skills for healthy social-emotional development.

KEY COMPONENTS OF SOCIAL-EMOTIONAL LEARNING (AS OUTLINED BY CASEL)

Self-Awareness: Through SEL, students strengthen their abilities to recognize and name personal emotions. Remind students that all feelings are acceptable and that they all communicate something to us. Self-awareness also includes the ability to understand our own needs, as well as our strengths and limitations. With self-awareness comes self-acceptance.

Self-Management: Self-management is the ability to regulate our emotions and behaviors so that they don't interfere with our goals. The coping skills taught in this book can help students manage their feelings and behaviors more effectively. Encourage every effort students make to manage their own emotions and behaviors, as this can be very difficult to do, especially at first.

Social Awareness: This is the ability to understand what others are feeling and to try to see their perspective. It allows us to relate to others, empathize with them, and see things from their points of view. Exercises aimed at improving social skills and awareness are included throughout this book. Encourage social curiosity, understanding, and respect.

Relationship Skills: Children need to be able to form positive social relationships, work together, and deal effectively with conflict. When children are intentionally taught social skills, given opportunities to practice, and provided guidance in teachable moments, they develop positive peer relationships, acceptance, and friendships.

Responsible Decision-Making: When young children learn to make positive choices about their personal and social behavior, they make responsible decisions. Many of the skills and activities in this book focus on problem-solving and making "wise decisions." Encourage students to *pause*, notice what is happening inside and around them, and then make a wise decision about what to do next.

About This Book

This book was developed so you can easily and effectively integrate mindfulness and SEL into your classroom experience. We designed each lesson to be completed within about fifteen minutes with very little preparation. The intent of this book is to teach mindfulness and social-emotional awareness in a way that is accessible, practical, and realistic for you and your students. Our hope is that as you move through these lessons, your students will develop greater awareness, self-acceptance, empathy, and compassion. By the end, we hope that you will discover you have nurtured a kinder, more tolerant community.

How This Book Is Organized

This book includes thirty lessons aimed at teaching mindfulness and social-emotional awareness. The lessons are organized around ten specific life skills, the core skills we believe are essential for developing mindfulness and social-emotional growth in the five areas of self-awareness, self-management, social awareness, relationship skills, and responsible decision-making. Each life skill section is divided into three lessons: Pause, Cope, and Connect. Here, we've outlined what you can expect from each of the life skill sections and their three related Pause, Cope, and Connect lessons.

Life Skills

Each life skill is a particular theme supported by current research in SEL, mindfulness, and/or the development of a growth mindset. At the start of each life skill section is a brief explanation of the skill and its benefits for children. We then offer a few recommendations for ways to introduce the life skill to students, devoting as much or as little time as you wish. Picture books make a good entry point, even with older students.

Lesson Types

All the lessons utilize mindfulness, but each Pause lesson is specifically focused on teaching students essential/core/foundational mindfulness skills. The Cope lessons focus on giving students strategies for dealing with difficult emotions. Lastly, the Connect lessons build on the foundation of the previous two lessons to teach interpersonal and social skills.

MINDFULNESS ACTIVITY (PAUSE)

Each Pause lesson is a mindfulness activity specifically related to the section's life skill. These lessons also teach the basic skills for practicing mindfulness. The Pause lessons are designed to work for a variety of learning styles, ranging from activities that are quieter and inwardly focused to ones that are expressive and interactive. The mindfulness practices in each Pause lesson might seem very simple, or they may seem less effective than expected or desired at first. Remember that mindfulness is best learned through repetition and will prove effective in dealing with life issues outside of the time students are practicing it in your classroom. In other words, you may not see immediate effects, but if you and your students continue to use the activities over time, you may see significant impact on students' self-regulation.

COPING SKILLS (COPE)

Applying the mindfulness skills they learn during the Pause lessons, students will learn to use coping skills to deal with common everyday challenges. The coping skills taught throughout this book are based on proven strategies for dealing with the issues addressed or similar scenarios.

INTERPERSONAL AND SOCIAL SKILLS (CONNECT)

The Connect lessons focus on developing positive social skills and fostering healthy relationships with peers within the context of the section's life skill. Some of the Connect lessons teach interpersonal skills, such as using "I" statements. Other activities and skills in these lessons are meant to foster a sense of social support and community, such as the Three Cs of Community or Kind Community lessons. The Connect lessons in this book should improve social skills and promote a positive classroom community.

Lesson Structure

Each lesson is organized in this way:

Lesson Summary. A brief description of what the lesson involves and intends to teach.

Keywords. Key terms that students should know and understand by the end of the lesson.

Students Will. Learning objectives for the lesson.

Materials. A list of materials you will need to conduct the lesson, if any, including the reproducible handouts.

Preparation. Instructions on preparing materials or the classroom before the lesson, if applicable.

Mindful Check-In. A brief mindfulness practice that can be a done before the main lesson. See a more detailed description in the "Conducting the Lessons and Working with Students" section of this introduction (page 11) and in "Mindful Pauses to Begin and End Lessons," which follows this introduction (page 17).

Activity. This includes an introduction or brief discussion followed by the learning activity itself, which may include step-by-step instructions or a suggested script.

Wrap-Up. A brief summary of the key learning points of the activity.

Mindful Checkout. A closing activity for the lesson. This is a fun way for students to self-evaluate their response to the activity. See a more detailed description in the "Conducting the Lessons and Working with Students" section of this introduction and in "Mindful Pauses to Begin and End Lessons," which follows this introduction.

Follow-Up. Suggestions for reinforcing the lesson's main skills or concepts in the following weeks or months.

Variations. Any possible variations or extensions to the activity that you may want to incorporate.

Considerations. Notes on adapting lessons for some student needs and concerns. These do not touch on all potential issues, but are intended to offer guidance on making the activities as inclusive as possible.

Handouts. Any handouts used in a lesson will immediately follow that lesson. You can photocopy the handouts or download and print them. (See page 186 for info on downloading.)

Additional Information

Resources. A selection of recommended books, websites, and other resources you may find helpful in learning and teaching students about mindfulness and SEL, as well as instructions for contacting the authors with any follow-up questions or concerns.

Digital Content. The digital content includes all the reproducible forms from the book, bonus life skills and lessons, and forms for sharing information with parents. See page 186 to access the digital content.

Using the Book in Your Setting

Yours may be one of the many classrooms where an SEL curriculum is already being implemented or where mindfulness has been introduced to students. The lessons in this book coincide with the concepts and skills taught in most SEL and school-based mindfulness programs. So if you've already been teaching SEL, you may want to be more selective in choosing the life skill areas to cover based on what students have already learned or on specific goals of your program. However, we encourage you to teach students Life Skill III, Pause. It's a foundational mindfulness skill that is also referenced in many other lessons in this book. After teaching the Pause lessons, you may select different life skills to focus on depending on your classroom needs and characteristics. The three lessons within each life skill build from first to last, so all three are best taught in sequence.

If your school or classroom doesn't have an SEL or mindfulness curriculum in place, we recommend going through the life skills and lessons in order. This will ensure that students build a foundation in the first few sections, helping them move through the later lessons in the book.

Making Time to Pause, Cope, and Connect

This book was developed to be flexible and adaptable for various student needs and settings. Lessons were also designed with an understanding of the time limits many teachers face, with a goal of each lesson taking an average of fifteen minutes or so.

Depending on your classroom's time constraints, there are a few different ways to build the lessons in this book into your curriculum:

- One lesson per week: One day, introduce the life skill and continue on to the first lesson (Pause). Then proceed to the next lesson (Cope) during the next week, followed by the third lesson (Connect) the week after that. Repeat for each life skill.

  □ Approximate time commitment per week: fifteen minutes

  □ Time to complete all lessons: thirty weeks

- One life skill per week: Each week, introduce a new life skill, then teach each of the three related lessons (Pause, Cope, and Connect) spread out in fifteen-minute lessons throughout the week.

  □ Approximate time commitment per week: forty-five minutes to an hour

  □ Time to complete all lessons: ten weeks

- You can also pick and choose the life skills that seem most relevant to your class based on students' maturity and the needs of the classroom. Here again, if you choose this option, we suggest you first teach the three lessons for the Pause life skill so that foundational practice is developed before integrating new life skills.

Conducting the Lessons and Working with Students

Before you begin, consider the following suggestions to enhance the experience you and your students have with the lessons.

Whiteboard, smart board, or chart paper. Many lessons in this book call for a whiteboard or other means of writing diagrams, acronyms, student ideas, and more in a place where students can see them. We don't include these in the lists of materials, as most classrooms have some form of displaying teachers' writing for all students. If you don't have a board available to write on, we recommend having a flip chart easel and chart paper on hand.

Wisdom Circle. Some lessons are most effective if done in a circle. This allows students to face each other. If children spend a lot of time in front of screens and interacting with each other via text, they may be limited in their abilities to read social cues or may feel awkward and anxious when engaged in face-to-face communication. You may choose to name your circle the Wisdom Circle, as they'll be learning more about themselves and each other while in it. We realize that this may not be feasible to do in every classroom. Try to make what accommodations you can to foster direct, face-to-face communication when possible.

Work in pairs and groups. Interacting in pairs or small groups enables kids to put the social skills and cooperative behaviors they are learning into action. Working together also helps kids develop feelings of comfort and safety in sharing feelings with each other.

Bell or chime. Since many of these lessons include guided mindfulness activities, it can be helpful to have a bell, chime, or singing bowl. There are also many cell phone apps that provide a range of chime and bell sounds.

The Pause. The Pause is a foundational skill for *Teaching Kids to Pause, Cope, and Connect.* It is taught as the third life skill in the book. Once students have learned the basic steps, you can guide them through the Pause in one to two minutes. The steps for the Pause are outlined in the "Mindful Pauses to Begin and End Lessons" guide that appears after this introduction.

The Pause integrates key skills, including body-calming strategies, mindful awareness, and Wise Action. Children (and adults) often react on autopilot or impulsively. The intention of the Pause is to help children "push the Pause button" between an event and their response. With repetition, the Pause can become automatic. As a result, when students are faced with upsetting situations, it is more likely that they will breathe, notice what they are thinking and feeling, then respond wisely, rather than react impulsively.

Soft ball. You may want to use a soft ball for students to pass around the circle or classroom to indicate whose turn it is to talk. You can also use any other talking object that works for your class.

Posters. Some of the activities include creating lists and posters with students, and some activities include key concepts that will be referenced in future lessons or in practicing mindfulness more broadly. You may want to put these on poster board or laminate them and post them around the classroom, so the skills and lessons are reinforced throughout the year. Some possible charts and posters to hang up in the classroom include:

- The Three Cs of Community (from Lesson 3)
- Our Community Commitments (from Lesson 3)
- A list of the four steps involved in the Pause (from "The Pause" handout after Lesson 9)
- "How Are You Feeling Today?" poster (handout after Lesson 19). This is a poster showing faces/emojis of different emotions, possibly divided into the four feeling zones: Happy/Peaceful, Angry, Sad, and Scared.
- The Stress Meter (from Lesson 12)

Role-playing and mini plays. Several activities in this book include skits or mini plays. Role-playing allows students to practice the interpersonal and coping skills they are learning so they feel more prepared to use them in real situations. Students act out a range of scenes so they can observe the different skills in action. To facilitate these scenes, you should try to set aside a "performance" area facing the student audience.

Trauma-Informed Mindfulness and Social-Emotional Learning

Many students face a range of chronically stressful or traumatic experiences, ranging from community violence and poverty to loss and illness (physical and mental) of close family members. A trauma-informed approach to mindfulness and SEL considers these vulnerabilities and sensitivities that students may be experiencing. Some of the lessons in this book include a "Considerations" section. These sections will explore some possible concerns or obstacles that may be barriers to teaching the lesson to your class, as well as potential ways to adapt the lesson to accommodate certain student needs. These occasionally include possible aspects of the lesson that could bring up traumatic experiences. Of course, it's impossible to predict all possible triggers or student responses, and we encourage you to use your own knowledge of your students to adapt lessons as needed. Consult with your school counselor or psychologist for further guidance or if any concerns arise.

Some trauma-informed considerations to be aware of while teaching the lessons in this book include the following:

Sensory sensitivity. Certain sensory experiences may be anxiety-provoking to students who have experienced trauma. These can include closing their eyes, sudden loud sounds, or unexpected physical contact. Provide students with modifications for such activities. For example, they can keep their eyes open during guided meditations or practice a calm/quiet alternative, like reading a book or listening to music, for loud and highly stimulating activities.

Physical and emotional safety. Traumatized children can be easily upset by situations that feel physically or emotionally threatening. Several activities in this book are designed to calm this autonomic "fight, flight, or freeze" reaction. Set community rules that promote mutual acceptance and respect of boundaries (physical and interpersonal). Remind students that they do not have to talk about anything they are not comfortable sharing.

Extra help. The lessons in this book can help students cope with difficult life situations. As a result, students may share personal feelings and experiences. If students bring up particularly difficult experiences, provide them with a safe, appropriate space to share and process them, such as a time to meet with you privately or a referral to the school counselor.

Common Questions and Concerns

You may have some concerns or reservations about teaching the lessons in this book, perhaps based on your experience or your school setting. You may also encounter certain challenges depending on your particular class and students' characteristics. We have tried to identify several possible concerns below and provided our suggestions and recommendations.

What if I have no experience with mindfulness? We wrote this book precisely with you in mind. You can teach the lessons without any prior experience with mindfulness. Carefully reading the introductory material and previewing each lesson will give you the grounding you need.

How do I lead mindfulness activities? We've provided sample scripts you can follow as you lead the guided mindfulness activities in this book. You may notice that the scripts include intentional pauses, unlike typical lessons.

What if some students are restless or resistant during activities? This can happen, and it is okay. Remind students that mindfulness is about learning to sit with our experiences, even if they're uncomfortable. For example, if a student says they're bored, encourage them to sit with that boredom. If students continue to be resistant, do not force them to participate. Instead, provide them with space to do something else quietly, like drawing, reading, or listening to music.

What if students share difficult emotions or experiences? One of the goals of SEL is accepting and working through various feelings, even those that are uncomfortable. The lessons in this book are intended to gradually help students increase their emotional awareness and coping skills. Let students know that they never have to share something if they aren't comfortable doing so and that they always have the option of sitting out of a lesson if it feels too difficult. If students express feelings or experiences that are concerning, be sure to consult with your school counselor or psychologist.

What if students have learning differences, struggle with reading or writing, or have other limitations? We have designed many of the activities so they can be conducted with minimal reading and writing required. Most of the student handouts offer the option of drawing or writing responses. We have also included some notes on possible considerations and modifications within the text.

From Mindful Awareness to Healthy Communities: The Pause, Cope, and Connect Continuum

If you are reading this book, you must have some curiosity about mindfulness and SEL and how these approaches might support the young people in your life (or even yourself). You may still be skeptical about how simply paying attention to your breath or mindfully eating a raisin can lead to greater emotional, mental, and physical well-being. How can these techniques help students who are perpetually distracted or students who argue with each other daily?

We encourage you to trust in the process. The research on both mindfulness and SEL increasingly demonstrates their effectiveness. This curriculum helps students gradually develop competencies in the interconnected domains of mindfulness (Pause), coping skills (Cope), and social skills (Connect). You should begin to see benefits in each of these areas within a few weeks. However, each of these competencies takes time and practice before students can use them proficiently or remember them during stressful situations. Over time, tools like the Pause will become more automatic, and students will become used to observing their feelings before acting on them. The SEL components of the curriculum will teach students to identify their feelings and work through difficult emotions rather than avoid them. With this increased self-awareness and self-acceptance, you will find that students will also become more accepting of each other. Despite the challenges children today face, they have the resources to be emotionally healthy, socially supportive, and resilient. If you are patient with the process, we believe the lessons in this book can help you guide your students in that direction. Kindness and compassion can be contagious.

We welcome your feedback and suggestions regarding this book and the ways in which it's supported you in your setting. We want to find the best ways possible to support other professionals and the children they serve. At the back of this book, we have provided contact information for reaching out to us with your feedback, questions, and concerns. You can also connect with us here:

Mark Purcell and Kellen Glinder
c/o Free Spirit Publishing
9850 51st Avenue, Suite 100
Minneapolis, MN 55442
help4kids@freespirit.com

Thank you for sharing our commitment to help children not only survive but thrive.

MiNDFUL Pauses to BEGiN aND END LESSONS

A brief mindfulness routine at the beginning and end of each lesson in this book can help students prepare to start the lesson or to move on from it by calming their physical activity and their thoughts. A consistent and brief mindfulness practice can develop into a habit for students when done repeatedly. These routines are highly customizable based on the classroom environment and the mix of personalities present on any given day. Here, we offer suggestions for ways to guide children through mindful pauses, helping them calm their minds and bodies before beginning each lesson (mindful check-in). A similar routine to conclude each lesson (mindful checkout) provides an extra opportunity for students to solidify what they have learned before moving on to their next activity.

Mindful Check-In
Mini Mindfulness Script
You can use the following script as a mindful check-in at the beginning of each lesson to help students practice mindfulness and be present for the lesson.

Sit comfortably and notice your body settle down.

Let go of what you were doing before this.

Breathe normally. Pay attention to your breath as it comes in and goes out.

Breathe in . . . breathe out . . . That's one breath.

Count your breaths up to four.

Pause for students to take four breaths. **When you reach four breaths, focus your attention on me.**

Notice how your body feels right now.

The Pause

The Pause is another mindful check-in option. Once students learn the Pause, we recommend using it as a mindful check-in for each lesson in this book to reinforce the practice and help students build a habit. To use the Pause for a mindful check-in, follow the steps below.

Invite students to find a comfortable position and close their eyes or gently gaze downward. Guide them through the Pause:

1. *STOP.* Stop; take a breath; observe; proceed.

2. *4 × 4 × 4 Breath:* Exhale to the count of four. Inhale to the count of four. Repeat four times.

3. *Mindful Detective:* Ask: **What signals are you getting from your body?** Pause. **What are you feeling?** Pause. **What are you thinking?** Pause.

4. *Wise Action:* Ask: **What should you choose to do?** Students may not have something immediate to *do.* So you may suggest they prepare to sit quietly and pay attention.

Ask students to open their eyes if closed. They can wriggle their fingers. Then begin the lesson. (The Pause can also serve as a mindful checkout; see "Practice the Pause" on page 19. If you're using the Pause for a mindful checkout, move on to the next activity of the students' day.)

Mindful Checkout

At the end of each lesson, you can do a mindful checkout to help students consolidate their learning and prepare to transition to their next activities. Invite students to find a comfortable position and sit quietly. Then, guide them through one of the following mindful checkout activities.

Practice Breath Awareness

Guide students through the Mini Mindfulness Script (use the script under "Mindful Check-In"). After students have taken four breaths, ask them to notice how their bodies and minds feel at that moment. Then move on to the next task.

Be Mindful of Change

This mindful checkout has students pause to notice how they feel at the end of the lesson compared to how they felt at the beginning. This is a simple way for students to notice changes they experienced as a result of the lesson and a way for you to assess the effect of the activity on members of the group.

Begin by asking students to sit comfortably and notice what they are thinking and feeling in their bodies. Ask them to consider how they felt before the lesson and to notice how they feel now. To add fun and creativity to the checkout, suggest a playful checkout metaphor, which can change with each lesson. Introduce a category for students to use as a metaphor (such as an animal or a color), asking them to describe how they felt before and after using items from that category.

For example, you could prompt students by saying, "Describe how you felt before and after the lesson as . . . animals." Demonstrate this by sharing your own description first. For example, you might say, "Before this lesson, I was feeling a little stressed and racing around—like a squirrel. Now, after practicing belly breathing with all of you, I feel relaxed and sleepy—like a bear getting ready to hibernate." Summarize the comparison: "Coming in, stressed squirrel. Now, hibernating bear." Then ask students to give their own descriptions using animal metaphors. One student might say that he felt angry like a growling lion before the lesson. But afterward, he may feel calm and confident like a soaring eagle.

Keeping metaphors to one category rather than leaving it open-ended provides students with guidance and structure, as well as a way to compare their metaphors and relate to each other. This is a fun way for students to share their experiences and build connections. As they get used to it, students may suggest their own categories of metaphors. Here are some categories you could use:

- animals
- colors
- weather
- types of food
- types of flowers
- insects
- environments in nature (ocean, mountains, forest)
- cartoon/video game characters

Practice the Pause

Once students learn the skills for the Pause, you may choose to practice it as both the mindful check-in and mindful checkout. This repetition can help children master the skill, so it becomes more automatic and accessible when they are distressed. To use the Pause for a mindful checkout, follow the steps listed on page 18.

LIFE SKILLS FOR TEACHING KIDS TO

PAUSE, COPE,
AND CONNECT

LIFE SKILL I
BE PRESENT

Mindfulness is the practice of purposely **focusing your attention on the present moment**—and accepting it without judgment. When kids notice their thoughts drifting and then bring their attention back to the breath, it can help them build focus. Every time they catch themselves before reacting to a thought, it can help build self-control. Mindfulness can also help kids become more self-aware and gain self-esteem.

Introducing This Life Skill to Students

There are different options for introducing the Be Present life skill based on the needs of your group and your time limitations. The following introductory activities provide learning experiences related to being present. If you are short on time, you can move ahead and start with Lesson 1 on page 25. Otherwise, you can introduce the skill with quotations and class discussion or by reading related books.

1. **Quotations and Socratic Questioning:** You may start a brief discussion by reading one of the quotations listed below (or another one chosen by you).

   - "Yesterday is history; tomorrow is a mystery. But today is a gift. That is why it is called the present." —Master Oogway from the film *Kung Fu Panda* (among others)

   - "Life is available only in the present moment." —Thich Nhat Hanh (paraphrased)

   - "There is only one time that is important—Now! It is the most important time because it is the only time when we have any power." —Leo Tolstoy

Follow up your chosen quotation with questions such as:

- What does this quote mean to you?
- This quote is about being present. What do you think it means to be present?
- Why do you think it is important to focus on the present moment?
- Can you share a time when you used the skill of being present?

2. **Related Literature:** You may wish to connect this life skill to relevant children's literature. You can begin a lesson by reading one of the children's books listed below, or you can read parts of it between the three lessons related to this life skill. Discuss how the characters or stories were about being present.

- *Here and Now* by Julia Denos
- *What Does It Mean to Be Present?* by Rana DiOrio

Further Resources

- "How Kids Can Benefit from Mindfulness Training" by Hilary A. Marusak, theconversation.com/how-kids-can-benefit-from-mindfulness-training-151654
- "What Is Diaphragmatic Breathing?" by Tim Jewell and Crystal Hoshaw, healthline.com/health/diaphragmatic-breathing

LESSON 1
WATCH YOUR FEELINGS SETTLE (PAUSE)

Lesson Summary

This first lesson serves as an introduction to the essential skill taught in this book: using mindfulness to develop awareness and cope with feelings. First, the connection between strong feelings and behaviors is discussed. Then, the glitter jar activity demonstrates the mindfulness practice of simply noticing feelings and watching them settle down on their own.

Keywords

- comfortable and uncomfortable feelings
- healthy and unhealthy behaviors
- mindfulness

Students Will

- understand how feelings can become very strong and even overwhelming
- learn how we can use healthy and unhealthy behaviors to cope with strong feelings
- learn that simply noticing these strong feelings, without doing anything, allows those feelings to settle down on their own

Materials

- two different colored markers for writing on whiteboard or other display

- quart-size glass or plastic jar with lid
- water, eco-friendly glitter glue (clear glue also works), and colorful biodegradable glitter
- *optional*: hot glue gun
- *optional*: *Moody Cow Meditates* by Kerry Lee MacLean

Time Constraints

This introductory lesson is a little longer than others in this book. If you're short on time, you can skip reading *Moody Cow Meditates* or spread the lesson across two days.

Preparation

MAKE THE GLITTER JAR

1. Pour ½ cup of water into the jar.
2. Pour ½ cup of glitter glue or clear glue into the jar.
3. Add 1–2 teaspoons of glitter to the jar.
4. Fill up the remainder of the jar with water.
5. *Optional*: To seal the glitter jar, use a hot glue gun to squeeze a ring of glue around the inside of the lid before securing it to the jar.

MOODY COW MEDITATES

If you have time to fit a picture book into your lesson, get a copy of the book *Moody*

Cow Meditates by Kerry Lee MacLean. This is an excellent picture book to teach mindfulness and managing feelings using the same metaphor of the glitter jar from this activity. However, if you don't have time or students are too old for the book, you can skip this part of the activity.

Mindful Check-In

Use the Mini Mindfulness Script in "Mindful Pauses to Begin and End Lessons" on page 17 to guide students through a mindful check-in. This helps students practice mindfulness and be present for the activity.

Activity

If you aren't reading *Moody Cow Meditates*, skip to the next paragraph. If you choose to begin by reading *Moody Cow Meditates*, explain that you are first going to read a book about feelings and mindfulness. Read the book to the students, or have them take turns reading aloud. Afterward, ask: **What were some of the Big Feelings Moody Cow had in the book? What were some of the things he did? What did his grandpa teach him to do with the glitter jar?**

Explain: **Now we're going to look at some of the Big Feelings we have in our own lives and what we do with them.** Ask students to name as many different feelings as they can, and write them down on the whiteboard. Write them all over the board rather than in a list. Explain: **Some of these feelings may feel comfortable, but others might feel uncomfortable to us.** Ask students to identify the feelings on the board that may feel comfortable, then the feelings that feel uncomfortable.

Say: **Sometimes feelings can get so big we don't know what to do with them.** Ask students to name some of the feelings that get big in their lives, underlining those the students identify. Explain: **When feelings get too big or out of control, we sometimes *do* something without thinking first. The things we *do* are our behaviors.**

Ask for examples of some of the things kids do when feelings get too big for them. Write these down in a different color marker than the feelings are written in. Write the behaviors haphazardly over the emotions. Many students may confuse feelings and behaviors, and labeling them with the appropriate color can help keep the class oriented. If someone reports they felt like hugging their dog, help them identify that hugging the dog is a behavior. Asking students what feeling might lead to that behavior, or what feelings that behavior might create, can highlight the differences between emotions and actions.

Say: **When we feel a big, hard-to-handle feeling, we might do something that seems to help us at the moment—but it actually makes things worse. We are going to call those unhealthy behaviors.** Refer students to the words on the board, and ask them to identify which behaviors seem healthy or unhealthy. Elicit a few more examples of healthy and unhealthy behaviors, continuing to write the behaviors in the second color marker over the feelings.

By the time you finish, the whiteboard should look like a mess with a range of behaviors jumbled up with different feelings. Say: **Out-of-control feelings can lead to out-of-control behaviors,**

which can lead to more out-of-control feelings. **How does it feel for you when this happens?** Invite responses. Refer to jumbled mess of words on the board. Say: **Our feelings and behaviors can be a jumbled mess.**

Provide some examples of this cycle of out-of-control feelings and behaviors, such as the scenario below:

1. You **feel mad** at recess, then **shove** a classmate.

2. Then you're sent to the principal, and you **feel angry and guilty and scared** about what your parents might say.

3. Your parent grounds you from electronics for what happened at school. You **feel mad**, and you **smash your game controller**, which leads to you being in more trouble.

4. By the end of the day, you **feel awful.**

Summarize: **We all have strong feelings sometimes. But you can learn to handle Big Feelings in positive ways. It begins with mindfulness. In our class, we'll be learning many different ways to practice mindfulness.**

Set the glitter jar on a table where all the students can see it. If you used *Moody Cow Meditates* to introduce the lesson, ask students: **In the book, how did Moody Cow learn to use the glitter jar?**

Say: **Imagine that the water in this jar is your mind and body. It starts each day clear and calm. But strong feelings can sometimes take over, like a storm of feelings.**

Lightly shake the jar until the water is clouded with colorful glitter. Continue:

When this happens, your mind is not clear, and your body is not calm. You can't think straight and may feel out of control. And remember, these out-of-control feelings can lead to out-of-control behaviors. In these moments, there is something you can do: you can wait and watch as the storm settles.

Set the jar down and allow the glitter to settle to the bottom. Say: **When you feel strong emotions, if you just watch them, without acting on them, they will settle down. Then you'll be able to think more clearly. Your body and feelings will calm down. This is called *mindfulness*. Mindfulness is the practice of carefully watching the feelings happening inside of us without acting on them—without doing anything.**

Refer students back to the whiteboard and the mess of feelings and behaviors written there. Say: **Let's practice doing this with one of the Big Feelings we listed.**

Ask students to sit in a comfortable position. Use the script below to guide them through the activity.

1. **Notice your body touching the seat or floor. Breathe a deep breath into your belly, then let it out. Bring your attention to right now. Let go of any thoughts about things that happened before or what you might do later.** Pause.

2. **Now breathe normally. Notice your breath as you breathe in . . . and out.** Pause.

3. Direct students to the feelings scribbled on the whiteboard. Invite them to silently pick one. Pause.

4. **Imagine having that feeling. You might even think about the last time**

you felt that feeling. If you want, shut your eyes to imagine that time in your mind. Pause.

5. **Imagine the feeling like a storm inside of you. Focus on how it feels inside your body. Notice where in your body you feel it and how it feels. Does your body feel hot or cold? Tense or shaky?** Pause.

6. **Now, open your eyes, and pay attention to the glitter jar.**

7. Shake up the glitter jar until the glitter is swirling around inside.

8. **Imagine that this glitter is the storm of feelings you have inside.** Pause.

9. **Watch the glitter in the jar. Notice your feelings inside.** Pause.

10. **Imagine your feelings settling down, just like the glitter.**

11. Wait for the glitter to settle to the bottom of the jar, allowing students to imagine their emotions settling.

Wrap-Up

Ask students to share how that experience was for them. Encourage students to describe how their feelings slowly changed and how they felt different in their bodies as they watched the glitter settle.

Summarize: **Our feelings are always changing. Sometimes they can feel very strong and out of control. At those times, we may act without thinking to try and get rid of the feeling. But if we can learn to just sit with those feelings and watch them, they will settle down like the glitter in the jar. Mindfulness is the practice of watching feelings and** learning from them instead of acting on them without thinking.

Mindful Checkout

Invite students to find a comfortable position and sit quietly. Choose one of these activities to guide your students through a mindful checkout, referencing "Mindful Pauses to Begin and End Lessons" on page 17 for guidance as needed:

- Practice Breath Awareness
- Be Mindful of Change

Follow-Up

You can keep the glitter jar in a particular place in the classroom. When you notice students having strong emotions, you may direct them to the glitter jar and have them practice letting their feelings settle down.

Variations

Give Students Take-Home Glitter Jars

If you choose, you can fill smaller jars with water and glitter for students to bring home with them. When you make the smaller glitter jars, follow the recipe under Preparation and adjust the quantities proportionately, noting that the ratios do not need to be exact. Since it can be distracting to play with the glitter jars, we suggest handing these out to students at the end of the activity or at the end of the day rather than before beginning the activity.

Have Students Make Their Own Glitter Jars

This can take a bit more time but is a fun art activity for students. Provide each student with supplies for making their own glitter jar. You may choose to use small containers to make mini glitter jars. Simply adjust the quantities proportionately—the ratios do not need to be exact.

Guide them through the activity using the instructions below.

1. Pour ½ cup of water into the Mason jar.
2. Pour ½ cup of glitter glue or clear glue into the jar.
3. Add 1–2 teaspoons of glitter to the jar.
4. Fill up the remainder of the jar with water.
5. *Optional*: To seal the glitter jar, use a hot glue gun to squeeze a ring of glue around the lid before securing it to the jar.

LESSON 2
BELLY BREATHING (COPE)

Lesson Summary
Students learn the basic connections between the body, mind, and emotions. The lesson begins with a comparison between two types of breathing: rapid shallow breathing, which can create anxiety, and deep belly breathing, which is calming and grounding. Students then learn belly breathing, also known as diaphragmatic breathing, which can slow the heart rate and calm them rapidly.

Keywords
- deep breaths
- belly breathing
- calming
- inhale
- exhale

Students Will
- learn to breathe into their diaphragm (belly breathing) as a way to calm themselves

Mindful Check-In
Use the Mini Mindfulness Script in "Mindful Pauses to Begin and End Lessons" on page 17 to guide students through a mindful check-in. This helps students practice mindfulness and be present for the activity.

Activity
Remind students of the Big Feelings they named in the previous lesson. Ask students: **Where do we usually feel our feelings?** Discuss how feelings are often felt in the body. Ask for examples from students of how different feelings feel inside their bodies.

Explain: **Our bodies and minds communicate with each other. Feelings in your mind can make your body feel different ways. But you can also teach your body to manage these feelings. In this activity, we are going to learn an exercise you can do anywhere. In fact, you are doing it right now.**

Ask: **How often do you really pay attention to your breath?** After brief discussion, continue: **Paying attention to the breath is one of the oldest and most common tools to help us focus and improve mindful awareness. And it can be done anywhere and at any time. Do you know why?** Elicit responses like *Because our breath is always with us.*

Belly Breathing Activity
Each student should be seated comfortably. Have them rest one hand on their chest and the other on their stomach. Ask students to scan their bodies and notice how they feel.

Explain: **First, we're going to see how simple breathing can make us feel stressed or calm.** *Note: You may want to have students with asthma or other breathing challenges sit out of this part of the activity.*

Have students take ten to fifteen rapid breaths, breathing up high into their chest. They should watch the hand on their chest rise and fall as they breathe. Afterward, ask students to describe how they feel. You can have them hold out their hands and notice if their fingers are shaking slightly. Students will likely report feeling jittery or dizzy. Ask: **When your body feels this way, what kinds of feelings do you have?** Students may report feeling a little nervous or scared.

Next, tell students that you're going to teach them a way to breathe that can make them feel calm and focused. Say: **Deep belly breathing is something athletes and performers use to help them feel calm, focused, confident, and peaceful before a big game or performance. See if you notice the difference between the two types of breathing.**

1. Have students sit up tall, without tensing, and place both hands on their lower abdominal muscles, just below the navel.

2. Have them imagine a balloon in their belly that fills with air as they inhale.

3. Together, take a slow, deep breath all the way down into the imaginary balloon. This should be a peaceful, quiet breath. Gently hold the breath in for a few seconds.

4. Now have students slowly, quietly, and gently breathe out, "deflating" the imaginary balloon as they exhale.

5. Repeat three times, extending the time of each exhalation.

6. After three deep breaths, have students remove their hands from their bellies and place them on their laps. Have them take two more deep breaths.

7. Instruct them to take a few regular breaths and roll their shoulders and stretch their necks to relieve any tension.

Wrap-Up

Ask students how they feel. Ask whether they noticed a difference between belly breathing and fast breathing. Discuss. Explain: **Belly breathing can help you remain calm when you have to do something you feel nervous about, like a test. It can also help you calm yourself down when you begin to get mad or upset.**

Mindful Checkout

Invite students to find a comfortable position and sit quietly. Choose one of these activities to guide your students through a mindful checkout, referencing "Mindful Pauses to Begin and End Lessons" on page 17 for guidance as needed:

- Practice Breath Awareness

- Be Mindful of Change

- Repeat belly breathing: Ask students to place their hands on their abdomens and take three deep belly breaths. Have them notice how their bodies and minds feel after these breaths.

Follow-Up

In the days that follow this lesson, you may want to start each day with a few belly breaths or take a pause for belly breathing during the day. You can also encourage students to take a few belly breaths when they are upset about something. With practice, many students will develop a healthy habit of breathing this way when under stress. Making students aware of this goal can help them solidify the habit.

Variation

Watch an Object Rise and Fall with the Breath

For this variation, you will need enough space for students to lie down. Ask them to place an object on their chest, such as a cup or balled-up piece of paper. Have them try to keep the object still as they do their belly breathing. You can also suggest they do this at home, in bed, with a favorite stuffed animal.

LESSON 3
THE THREE Cs OF COMMUNITY (CONNECT)

Lesson Summary

In this lesson, students create their own visual representation of their community based on the three Cs: the principles of caring, connecting, and contributing. Then, they will agree on commitments to make as a classroom community.

Keywords

- community
- caring
- connecting
- contributing
- commitments

Students Will

- learn three aspects of community: caring, connecting, and contributing
- create their own vision and guidelines for their classroom community

Materials

- three large pieces of paper to draw on, such as poster board, butcher paper, or flip chart paper
- drawing supplies
- "Our Community Commitments" handout (page 36)

Time Constraints

This lesson may take closer to twenty or twenty-five minutes. If you're short on time, spread the two parts of the lesson across two days. You can also discuss examples of the three Cs of community as a group rather than making posters, then move on to the second part of the lesson ("Our Community Commitments").

Preparation

Set up three areas in the classroom where groups can work on their posters, either on the floor or on large tables.

Mindful Check-In

Use the Mini Mindfulness Script in "Mindful Pauses to Begin and End Lessons" on page 17 to guide students through a mindful check-in. This helps students practice mindfulness and be present for the activity.

Activity

Ask students what is meant by the word *community*, and discuss their answers. Provide these two basic definitions of *community*:

1. *A group of people who live together or spend time together at the same place*

   Examples: neighborhood, school, or classroom

2. *A group of people who share a feeling of closeness because they have similar interests and goals*

   Examples: sports team, club or scouts, close friends

Explain: **We are all going to work together to create a picture of how we would like our classroom community to be. To do that, we are going to focus on the three Cs of community.**

On the whiteboard, write "Caring, Connecting, and Contributing." Ask for brief examples of each. Students may need some help understanding the term *contributing*. Explain that contributing is when you get involved and do something that helps the group.

Three Cs of Community Activity

Divide students into three groups. Provide each group with paper and drawing supplies to make their posters.

Assign one of the three Cs to each group: caring, connecting, and contributing.

Explain: **Work as a team to create a poster that shows how your assigned word (*caring, connecting,* or *contributing*) is part of being a community. Be creative. You can use words, symbols, or pictures to show what the word means to you.**

Go around the room and provide support to groups as they work on their posters. Encourage cooperation within each group. Allow ten minutes to complete the activity. Then ask groups to share their posters with the class.

Our Community Commitments Activity

Ask students to work in their small groups or individually to come up with ideas for possible classroom community commitments. Invite them to write their ideas on the first part of the "Our Community Commitments" handout (page 36). Students can use the three Cs of community as a starting point for their suggestions.

When groups have finished coming up with ideas, lead a large-group discussion. Collectively decide on five or six community commitments for the class and write them on the whiteboard. These can serve as guidelines for participation and mutual respect between students. Have the students write these commitments on the second half of the "Our Community Commitments" handout.

Wrap-Up

Say: **Working on these posters and commitments together was an activity that showed the three Cs of community. You each had to connect and contribute. And you had to care about each other and the projects while you did it.**

Have the groups hold the three posters together, or use magnets to spread them across the whiteboard. Say: **Together, these posters are a mural of our community.** If permitted, you may want to take a picture to show students later.

Mindful Checkout

Invite students to find a comfortable position and sit quietly. Choose one of these activities to guide your students through a mindful checkout, referencing "Mindful Pauses to Begin and End Lessons" on page 17 for guidance as needed:

- Practice Breath Awareness
- Be Mindful of Change

Follow-Up

Keep the students' posters of the three Cs of community for later lessons (specifically for the final life skill in this book, Be Kind). If you choose, you can hang up the three posters. If groups did not finish their posters, you can allow them to work on them during breaks or free time. Encourage students to add to the posters of the three Cs throughout the week.

If conflicts happen during the coming weeks, remind students of their community commitments. Encourage them to act in a way that leads to a more positive classroom community.

OUR COMMUNITY COMMITMENTS

In the space below, write down some ideas for commitments your class could make as a group. These commitments could focus on respect, participation, the three Cs of community (caring, connecting, and contributing), or any other values or policies you'd like to have in your class.

Write down the community commitments you and your classmates decided on.

Name:_____ Date:_____

From *Teaching Kids to Pause, Cope, and Connect: Lessons for Social-Emotional Learning and Mindfulness* by Mark Purcell, Psy.D., and Kellen Glinder, M.D., copyright © 2022. This page may be reproduced for individual, classroom, or small group work only. For other uses, contact Free Spirit Publishing at freespirit.com/permissions.

LIFE SKILL II
BE CURIOUS

?

Data on predictions of academic performance have shown that curiosity is one of the three key predictors of academic achievement, alongside intelligence and effort (von Stumm, Hell, and Chamorro-Premuzic 2011). Students with high levels of curiosity have reported greater life satisfaction, positive emotions, hope, and purpose in life (Eva 2018). One study found that undergraduate and graduate students with high levels of curiosity also demonstrate greater emotional intelligence (Leonard and Harvey 2007).

Curiosity is in many ways the catalyst for learning. From a young age, it is children's curiosity that drives them to ask what things are and incessantly ask, "But why?" It is at the heart of scientific inquiry and invention. Curiosity is considered fundamental in developing a growth mindset (rather than a fixed mindset). Encouraging students to be curious will enhance their imagination, critical thinking, and learning (Price-Mitchell 2015).

Researcher Amy L. Eva suggests new techniques for helping students develop curiosity in the classroom that you may wish to model in your teaching (2018):

Five Tips for Cultivating Curiosity

1. **Model risk-taking.**

   Some students may be avoiders. They struggle to tolerate the anxiety that comes with new experiences. Teachers can help them by modeling risk-taking regularly in the classroom.

2. **Normalize anxiety.**

   Teaching mindfulness and self-compassion gives students tools to help them tolerate stress and navigate the anxiety and frustration that may accompany new experiences.

3. **Provide challenging options for group projects.**

   Learning tasks should encourage curiosity. New and challenging tasks should be well-scaffolded to support student success. They should also center on group inquiry and higher-order questions and be supported by cooperative group structures.

4. **Link boring tasks with things that interest kids.**

Try to integrate learning tasks that may be less interesting with those that are more novel and memorable.

5. **Let curiosity drive goal-setting and growth.**

Curiosity fosters purpose and hope. Teachers can use curiosity as motivation for students' short- and long-term goals. Inquire about the subjects or interests that excite students at school (and beyond). Encourage them to learn more about the interests they dream of exploring, or careers that are most appealing.

Introducing This Life Skill to Students

There are several options for introducing the Be Curious life skill based on the needs of your group and your time limitations. The following lessons provide different learning experiences related to Being Curious. If you are limited on time, you can start with the first lesson. Otherwise, you can introduce the skill with quotations and class discussion or by reading related books.

1. **Quotations and Socratic Questioning:** You may start a brief discussion by reading one of the quotations listed below (or another one chosen by you).

   - "Think and wonder, wonder and think." —Dr. Seuss

   - "I have no special talent. I am only passionately curious." —Albert Einstein

   - "When you're curious, you find lots of interesting things to do." —Walt Disney

   Follow up your chosen quotation with questions such as these:

   - What does this quote mean to you?

   - How does it relate to the life skill of being curious?

   - Why do you think it is important to be curious?

   - Can you share a time when you were curious?

2. **Related Literature:** You may wish to connect this life skill to relevant children's literature. You can begin a lesson by reading the book listed below, or you can read parts of it between the three lessons related to this life skill.

   - *What Do You Do with an Idea?* by Kobi Yamada

Further Resources

- "How to Cultivate Curiosity in the Classroom" by Amy L. Eva, greatergood.berkeley .edu/article/item/how_to_cultivate_curiosity_in_your_classroom

LESSON 4
YOUR FIRST TASTE OF MINDFULNESS (PAUSE)

Lesson Summary

This lesson is a basic guided mindfulness activity to teach students about mindful eating. The practice of mindful eating provides a direct, sensory experience of being fully aware.

Keywords

- mindfulness
- mindful eating
- noticing
- describing

Students Will

- practice mindful eating
- learn basic principles of mindfulness

Materials

- bowl of raisins or another bite-size healthy food, such as cereal, corn chips, blueberries, or frozen peas
- spoon, fork, or tongs for serving food
- napkins or small plates

Preparation

Fill a bowl with your chosen healthy food (in this lesson, we will refer to raisins). Be aware of any food allergies and choose a food appropriate for all students.

Mindful Check-In

Use the Mini Mindfulness Script in "Mindful Pauses to Begin and End Lessons" on page 17 to guide students through a mindful check-in. This helps students practice mindfulness and be present for the activity.

Activity

Share this quotation from Master Oogway from *Kung Fu Panda* (and others), which you may have used when introducing the Be Present life skill: "Yesterday is history; tomorrow is a mystery. But today is a gift. That is why it is called the present." Ask students what they think this quote means. Say: **We've been learning ways to focus on our breathing and to be present. These skills are part of something called mindfulness. Focusing all your attention on what is happening in the present moment, both inside your body and around you, is one of the most important parts of mindfulness.**

Ask: **What do I mean by *the present moment*?** Elicit a response like *now* or *right now*.

Ask: **We can notice our thoughts, feelings, and *sensations* in our bodies. What do I mean by *sensations*?** Elicit a response like *physical feelings in our bodies*.

Ask: **What are the different types of senses we have?** Elicit the five senses: hearing, sight, smell, taste, and touch.

Explain: **Mindfulness is a special way of noticing, of being aware. It's a way of looking inside ourselves—a type of inner vision. It can help us understand ourselves better. Mindfulness focuses our attention on two important questions.** Write the following two questions on the whiteboard:

1. What is happening inside me and around me right now?

2. Can I stay with the experience without judging it?

Refer to the first question. Explain: **This means noticing what you are experiencing in each passing moment as it happens by paying attention to—focusing your awareness on—*right now.* This is mindful awareness.**

Next, help students experience mindful awareness of the present moment:

1. Invite students to settle into their seats and be aware of their bodies making contact with the chair or their feet making contact with the floor.

2. Ask students to either slowly shut their eyes or pick a spot and softly look downward. Demonstrate how to do this if needed.

3. Say: **Take a few deep breaths into your belly.** Pause. **Focus on what is happening right now. Listen to the following questions, and answer them silently to yourself:**

   • What are you sensing in your body?

   • What do you hear?

   • What are you thinking?

   • What are you feeling?

4. Encourage a few students to share their present-moment experience.

Explain: **Next, we're going to do an activity that uses the senses to practice mindfulness. It's called mindful eating. A lot of times, we eat so fast we barely notice what we are tasting or feeling in our bodies. The practice of mindful eating is a good way to use all our senses to be fully aware of what we are experiencing moment by moment.**

Serve students a few raisins each with a spoon, fork, or tongs. Ask the children not to eat the raisins yet.

Use this sample script to guide students through a mindful eating practice. You can adapt this script to meet your class's needs:

1. Look at the raisin as if it's your first time seeing it. Pretend you've just dropped in from Mars and you've never seen an object like this before. Explore every part of it.

2. **Notice how the raisin feels between your fingers. You may close your eyes while doing this.**

3. **Hold the raisin beneath your nose, and inhale through your nose. Notice how it smells. Notice sensations in your mouth or stomach.**

4. Now, slowly bring the raisin to your lips. Gently place it in your mouth. Without chewing, explore it with your tongue. Notice how it feels to have the food in your mouth.

5. When you are ready, take one or two bites into the raisin and notice what happens. What do you taste as

you chew? Does it feel different on your tongue now? Notice how it has changed.

6. Do you feel ready to swallow the raisin? What feeling tells you it's time to swallow? Notice that feeling before you swallow it.

7. Finally, see if you can feel the food moving down into your stomach. Notice how your body is feeling after mindful eating. What tastes or sensations are still in your mouth?

8. Continue to eat whatever food is left in the same way, practicing mindful eating.

When you have completed the mindful eating activity, ask students if this way of eating was different from how they typically eat. Ask what they noticed when they were paying mindful attention during the activity. Emphasize the two main areas of mindfulness practice: (1) focusing on the present moment and (2) observing and describing without judgment. Use questions like the following, which are important for processing all mindfulness activities:

1. **Were you able to stay in the present moment and focus on what you were thinking, feeling, hearing, tasting, smelling, and sensing in your body?**

   - Follow-up questions can be: **Were you thinking of what happened before the activity? Were you worried about anything in the future?** If not, then they were practicing mindfulness.

   - Explain: **It is normal for our minds to wander while we are trying to stay present. As soon as you notice your mind has**

wandered, bring it back to what you are trying to do in the present. In the last activity, that would be eating mindfully.

2. **Did any *judgments* come up in your mind while you were doing the activity?** Refer to the second question written on the whiteboard and underline the word *judgment*. Ask students what is meant by the word *judgment*. Elicit responses focused on using negative words to describe people, things, or experiences.

   - Explain: **The second part of mindfulness is to observe and describe your experience without judging it. If we do judge or label our experience, we should notice that too.** Permit students to express any judgments that may have come to mind during mindful eating (such as "This is dumb" or "This tastes gross"). Let students know that they will spend more time learning about judgments in the next lesson.

   - Explain: **Judgments can appear in our brain just like thoughts and emotions, and that's okay. The important thing is to simply notice the judgment, then come back to the present moment.**

   - Summarize: **Remember, the goal of mindfulness is to notice what is happening *right now*. With mindful eating, that meant noticing what you experienced through your senses, like taste, smell, and touch. Judgments or labels like "This tastes gross" can take you away from feeling what is actually happening in your body from moment to moment.**

Wrap-Up

Encourage students to ask any questions they may have about mindfulness and mindful eating. Let them know that they will have the chance to practice many different types of mindfulness activities in the days ahead. Reassure students that mindfulness is not about success or failure. Instead, it is about the practice. Briefly discuss other activities in their lives where practice helps them get better. Remind students that people aren't often good at something when they first try to do it. It takes practice. And mindfulness is the same.

Mindful Checkout

Invite students to find a comfortable position and sit quietly. Choose one of these activities to guide your students through a mindful checkout, referencing "Mindful Pauses to Begin and End Lessons" on page 17 for guidance as needed:

- Practice Breath Awareness
- Be Mindful of Change

Follow-Up

Encourage students to continue to practice one of the basic skills of mindfulness: observing and describing their experiences in the moment. Whenever possible, try to keep students focused on the present rather than the past or future.

Considerations

Be aware of any student allergies before beginning this lesson, and ensure the bite-size snack you serve is safe for all students. If necessary, you can have two types of food available.

LESSON 5
BE A DETECTIVE (COPE)

Lesson Summary

Students will practice noticing and describing objects as a way to grow in mindfulness. They will understand how noticing and describing differ from labeling and judging.

Keywords

- noticing
- describing
- labeling
- judging

Students Will

- learn how to notice what they see and describe it without using common labels
- learn that noticing and describing are important parts of mindfulness

Materials

- opaque containers with two or three different objects inside (such as a pebble, a coin, an eraser, a pine cone, a sponge)—prepare one container per group of four to five students.
- "Be a Detective" handout

Preparation

Set up areas where four to five students can work together in groups. Prepare one container per group.

Mindful Check-In

Use the Mini Mindfulness Script in "Mindful Pauses to Begin and End Lessons" on page 17 to guide students through a mindful check-in. This helps students practice mindfulness and be present for the activity.

Activity

Arrange students in small groups of four or five.

Ask: **What does a detective do?** Elicit responses like *gather clues*, *ask questions*, and *investigate*. Say: **A detective first notices what they see, hear, and feel. These are clues.**

Explain: **Mindfulness is like being a detective. The first step of mindfulness is to notice what we see, think, and feel inside and outside of us.** Take out one of the objects from the containers to be used for the activity. For example, you could take out a paper clip.

Say: **A detective's next step is to investigate.** Ask students to share what it means to investigate something. Ask for a volunteer, then hand them the object. Invite the volunteer to examine the object as much as possible.

Say: **The third step is to describe what you have observed.** Ask the volunteer to describe the object *without naming it*. For

example, the student may say it is small, cold, made of metal that looks silver, and bent in long loops.

Ask: **Does that tell you more about the object than simply calling it by its name?** In the above example, labeling it as a paper clip gives us a mental image but leaves out the observations that the object is cold or silver in color, for instance. It can be helpful to highlight the difference between observing characteristics of an object and naming the object by asking students specific questions such as "How does it feel or smell?" or "Is it bigger than your hand?"

Noticing Group Activity

1. Tell students that you are now going to let them be detectives in small groups. Give each group one of the containers. Ask students to keep the objects in the containers.

2. Distribute one "Be a Detective" handout to each group. Ask each group to pick one member to be the notetaker, who will write down what the group notices on the "Be a Detective" worksheet.

3. Ask each group to remove one object and place it on the table.

4. Invite them to describe the object in as much detail as possible without naming it. Students can pick the object up and touch it, smell it, or look closely at it.

5. The notetaker should write the group's observations down in the column labeled "Investigating an Object." They should write down as many details as possible.

6. After the group has recorded the details, they can return the object to the container and select another.

7. After about five minutes, have the groups return all objects to their containers.

8. Say: **Let's find out how you did as detectives. Who can describe what you observed?** Ask the notetaker from each group to pick one object and read the descriptions to the larger group. Say: **Who can guess the name of the object based only on the descriptions or "clues"?**

9. When students finish, congratulate them on being good investigators.

Explain: **Mindfulness is very similar to playing detective. When we are mindful, we notice and describe what we feel in our bodies and minds.**

Ask students to practice investigating their experience using their senses. Instruct them to pay attention to what they are feeling right now. Distribute blank "Be a Detective" handouts to each student (they can set aside the one completed as a group). Ask them to complete the second half of the handout, "Investigating My Experience." Alternatively, instead of having students fill out their own worksheets, you may guide students by reading the prompts aloud, pausing after each for students to notice what they are experiencing.

Afterward, ask for a few volunteers to share what they noticed or wrote. Provide encouragement and highlight areas where the student was descriptive.

Wrap-Up

Say: **A good detective tries to explain what they notice with as much detail as possible. In a good investigation, it is important not to make quick judgments and to get all the facts first.**

Explain: **The same is true with mindfulness. Practicing mindfulness means trying to notice as much as you can about what you are feeling, using all your senses, just like you did in this activity. Once you've done that, you can describe what you feel with as many details—or "clues"—as possible. Avoid labels or judgments. These take you away from what is happening here and now.**

Mindful Checkout

Invite students to find a comfortable position and sit quietly. Choose one of these activities to guide your students through a mindful checkout, referencing "Mindful Pauses to Begin and End Lessons" on page 17 for guidance as needed:

- Practice Breath Awareness
- Be Mindful of Change

Follow-Up

As often as possible, notice when students use labels or judgments, like "Math is stupid" or "Isla is a jerk." Privately encourage them to describe their experience instead. For example, the student could say instead, "I have a hard time understanding math," or, "My feelings were hurt when Isla didn't play with me at recess." These are excellent informal mindfulness practices for students to do regularly.

Variations
What Has Changed?

Divide students into pairs. Ask them to spend a few moments looking at each other. Then ask students to turn around so that they are facing away from each other. Have each student change three things about their appearance. Suggestions include: remove a necklace; switch wrists for a bracelet; untie a shoe lace; change hairstyle. Ask students to turn back around and try to figure out what has changed in their partner's appearance. Wrap up this version of the activity with a discussion about how easily we can miss noticing things around us.

Awareness Test

Show students the brief "Basketball Awareness Test" video at youtube.com/watch?v=Ahg6qcgoay4.

Be sure that your introduction to this video does not give away the mindfulness surprise to students who have not yet seen the video. Before showing it, ask students not to speak out loud as they "take the test." This fun video is a good example of how we tend to focus our attention on what we expect to see and miss other things going on.

Be A Detective

To be a detective, you need to:

1. Notice and Observe: Use all your senses.
2. Describe: Include as much detail as possible.

Investigating an Object	Investigating My Experience
Use all your senses to observe the object and describe what you notice (without naming it):	Use all your senses to observe what you are experiencing right now:
1. The object is....	I see:
	I smell:
	I hear:
2. The object is....	I taste:
	In my body, I feel:
3. The object is....	In my mind, I think:
	In my heart, I feel:

Name:_____ Date:_____

From *Teaching Kids to Pause, Cope, and Connect: Lessons for Social-Emotional Learning and Mindfulness* by Mark Purcell, Psy.D., and Kellen Glinder, M.D., copyright © 2022. This page may be reproduced for individual, classroom, or small group work only. For other uses, contact Free Spirit Publishing at freespirit.com/permissions.

LESSON 6
MINDFUL LISTENING (CONNECT)

Lesson Summary

In this lesson, students will learn to be actively engaged in listening to others through mindfulness.

Keywords

- mindful listening

Students Will

- learn how to listen to each other mindfully

Materials

- "Mindful Listening: Do You Hear Me?" handout

Mindful Check-In

Use the Mini Mindfulness Script in "Mindful Pauses to Begin and End Lessons" on page 17 to guide students through a mindful check-in. This helps students practice mindfulness and be present for the activity.

Activity

Explain that mindfulness isn't just useful for being present in your own life. It can also improve the way you relate to others. Remind students of the two basic parts of mindfulness: (1) staying present and (2) noticing and describing what is happening.

Say: **We are going to learn the difference between distracted listening and mindful listening.**

Ask for a student volunteer. Arrange two chairs so that you are facing the volunteer. Ask the student to tell you about their day. As the student talks, do several things that show that you are distracted, such as looking around the room, interrupting, walking away, and asking irrelevant questions. Do this for a few minutes.

When you end the conversation, ask: **What were some of the things I did that showed I was not listening very well?** Ask your volunteer how that felt for them.

Say: **Okay, let's try that again. This time, I will try to practice *mindful listening*.** With the same student, demonstrate the steps of mindful listening (listed in the "Mindful Listening" handout). When you have finished, ask students how that was different. Ask the student volunteer how that felt different.

Distribute the "Mindful Listening" handout, and read through the four steps. Tell students that they're now going to practice being mindful listeners.

1. Divide students into pairs.

2. Invite them to take turns, with one person being the listener and the other being the speaker.

3. Say: **For two minutes, I want one of you to be the speaker, and the**

other to be the mindful listener. The speaker may want to talk about their day or things they're interested in. Or the listener could start with a question like "What did you do last weekend?" The listener should listen mindfully to the speaker.

4. Read the four steps of mindful listening from the handout, and encourage students to use their handout during the activity:

   □ Look at the person who is speaking.

   □ Pay close attention to what the speaker is saying.

   □ Wait to talk until the person finishes speaking.

   □ Ask questions to understand how the person feels and what the person wants.

5. Circle the room as the pairs practice mindful listening. Provide constructive feedback.

6. After two minutes, ask the pairs to switch roles.

7. When the activity is finished, ask for volunteers to share something they learned about their partners.

Wrap-Up

Explain how important it can be to listen mindfully. Say: **When we listen mindfully, we can better understand what the other person is** *saying***. Even more important than that, we can better understand what the other person is** *feeling***.**

Mindful Checkout

Invite students to find a comfortable position and sit quietly. Choose one of these activities to guide your students through a mindful checkout, referencing "Mindful Pauses to Begin and End Lessons" on page 17 for guidance as needed:

- Practice Breath Awareness
- Be Mindful of Change

Follow-Up

During the upcoming days, try to encourage students to practice mindful listening with each other informally. You may ask them to try to paraphrase each other's comments when differing opinions arise in classroom discussions. If you do a classroom project or hold a class discussion, it can be helpful to have a group of students look for and identify mindful listening in others while the classroom discussion proceeds. Naming the skill of mindful listening as you or someone else is practicing this behavior can be a powerful reinforcement of this lesson.

THE FOUR STEPS OF MINDFUL LISTENING

1. Look at the person who is speaking.

2. Pay close attention to what the speaker is saying.

3. Wait to talk until the person finishes speaking.

4. Ask questions to understand how the person feels and what the person wants.

Name:_____ Date:_____

From *Teaching Kids to Pause, Cope, and Connect: Lessons for Social-Emotional Learning and Mindfulness* by Mark Purcell, Psy.D., and Kellen Glinder, M.D., copyright © 2022. This page may be reproduced for individual, classroom, or small group work only. For other uses, contact Free Spirit Publishing at freespirit.com/permissions.

LIFE SKILL III
PAUSE

We often react without thinking, as if we're on autopilot. But if we can learn to pause for even a few seconds between the time something happens and the moment when we react, it can make all the difference.

"Pressing the Pause button" between an event and a reaction gives children a chance to observe their emotions and surroundings, make a wise choice, and then continue in a better way. It allows them to use their understanding of their thoughts and emotions and what's happening around them to decide what to do.

Kids need to practice pressing the Pause button in order to build this muscle of awareness. We can help them practice by encouraging them to pause and breathe; be aware of the present moment; and notice what they are thinking, feeling, and doing. Reminding kids to press the Pause button teaches them to better regulate emotions, make wise decisions, and manage their behavior.

Introducing This Life Skill to Students

There are various options for introducing the Pause life skill based on the needs of your group and your time limitations. The following lessons provide learning experiences related to learning to Pause. If you are limited on time, you can start with the first lesson. Otherwise, you can introduce the skill with quotations and class discussion or by reading related books.

1. **Quotations and Socratic Questioning:** You may start a brief discussion by reading one of the quotations listed below (or another one chosen by you).

   • "Consider the Pause like a stop sign. It doesn't mean you stop forever. You stop, look around to increase your awareness of your surroundings, and proceed when it's safe to do so." —Darcy Luoma

- "Practice the pause. Pause before judging. Pause before assuming. Pause before accusing. Pause whenever you're about to react harshly and you'll avoid doing and saying things you'll later regret." —Lori Deschene

Follow up your chosen quotation with questions such as:

- What does this quote mean to you?
- How does it relate to the life skill of learning to Pause?
- Why do you think it is important to Pause?
- Can you share a time when you paused before acting?

2. **Related Literature:** You may wish to connect this life skill to relevant children's literature. You can begin a lesson by reading one of the books listed below, or you can read parts of it between the three lessons related to this life skill.

- *A World of Pausabilities: An Exercise in Mindfulness* by Frank J. Sileo
- *What Were You Thinking? Learning to Control Your Impulses* by Bryan Smith
- *My Magic Breath: Finding Calm Through Mindful Breathing* by Nick Ortner and Alison Taylor

Further Resources

- "Pressing Pause: How Mindfulness Helps Kids" by Deborah Farmer Kris, pbs.org/parents/thrive/pressing-pause-how-mindfulness-helps-kids

LESSON 7
PRESSING THE PAUSE BUTTON (PAUSE)

Lesson Summary

Students will learn the first two steps of the Pause exercise: the STOP acronym and 4 × 4 breathing, a core breathing practice.

Keywords

- STOP
- mindful breathing
- 4 × 4 breath, 4 × 4 breathing
- 4 × 4 × 4 breath, 4 × 4 × 4 breathing
- calming

Students Will

- learn the steps of STOP: **S**top, **T**ake a Breath, **O**bserve, **P**roceed
- learn to practice 4 × 4 and 4 × 4 × 4 breathing

Materials

- "STOP" handout
- "4 × 4 Breathing" handout

Mindful Check-In

Use the Mini Mindfulness Script in "Mindful Pauses to Begin and End Lessons" on page 17 to guide students through a mindful check-in. This helps students practice mindfulness and be present for the activity.

Activity

Explain: **We are going to learn the first steps of a very important skill called the Pause. It's sort of like pressing your own Pause button. Ask: Who can tell me what happens when you press a Pause button?**

Ask: **What would happen if you could press a Pause button in life?** Elicit some imaginative answers from students. **What about if you could press the Pause button when you were getting upset about something or when you were about to yell or do something out of control? How would pressing Pause change the situation?**

Explain: **The Pause is probably one of the most useful skills that you will learn from mindfulness. We're going to keep practicing it as we keep working on our mindfulness skills. The more you practice, the more prepared you will be to use it when you need it.**

STOP Activity

Write the word STOP vertically on the board.

Explain: **To begin this activity we need to first STOP: S-T-O-P.** Next to each letter, write the following:

S—Stop

T—Take a Breath

O—Observe

P—Proceed

Briefly walk through the steps of STOP and refer students to the "STOP" handout.

S—Stop: **Stop what you are doing.**

T—Take a Breath: **Take a deep belly breath.**

O—Observe: **Notice what is happening inside and outside of you.**

P—Proceed: *Proceed* **means to go ahead and do something. To proceed, think and decide on the best action to take next.**

Explain: **You can practice STOP at any time in your day to pause and make a mindful decision or turn your thoughts to the present moment. STOP is also the first step in the Pause. Now, we are going to practice the next step, a special kind of belly breathing.**

4 × 4 Breathing Activity

Explain: **Earlier, we learned how belly breathing can help us feel calm. Now, we are going to practice a special way of breathing called 4 × 4 breathing. This is a way to use belly breathing to calm our minds, our bodies, and our emotions. Calming ourselves in this way prepares us for deciding what action to take next.**

Explain the importance of this type of breathing by using the metaphor of a kite. Say: **As you try to pay attention to your breath, your mind may wander and get distracted. That is normal. As soon as you catch your mind wandering, gently bring your attention back to focus on your breath. Imagine your attention is a kite flying in the sky. The wind can blow your kite one way and another, just as your thoughts and emotions might bring your attention from one** emotion or sensation to another. The kite string keeps the kite in control. In a similar way, calming breaths can keep your attention and your mind in control. If a strong wind blows a kite, you focus on holding the string to keep the kite from flying away. When strong emotions or thoughts affect your mind, you can focus on your calming breath to keep your thoughts and emotions from moving out of control. Your breath is the kite string that gently pulls your mind back and keeps it from floating away.**

Give students the "4 × 4 Breathing" handout and read through the first part together. Then have students put their handouts down while you guide them:

1. Begin by practicing STOP for about ten seconds. Remind students to try to quiet their bodies and bring their attention to right now—the present moment.

2. Explain: **We are now going to focus our attention on our breathing. To start, you'll slowly** *exhale*—**meaning you'll breathe out slowly. When I say "Exhale," breathe out normally. As you gently breathe out, count to four in your head. While you're exhaling, imagine clearing away your thoughts, like clearing clouds from the sky. Notice your shoulders and chest relax as you breathe out. Imagine any stress or tightness draining out of your body each time you exhale.**

3. Continue: **Then you'll slowly** *inhale*—**meaning you'll breathe in slowly. When I say "Inhale," breathe in deeply while counting to four. Inhale as slowly as possible while still feeling comfortable. Try to breathe deep into your belly.**

4. Say: **This cycle of a four-count** *exhale* **followed by a four-count** *inhale* **is called a 4 × 4 breath. It always starts with** *ex*haling and ends **after** *in*haling: out first, then in.

5. **Let's begin: Ready . . . breathe out while counting to four in your head.**

6. When you're ready to inhale, take a deep belly breath in while counting silently to four.

Next, have students practice a 4 × 4 breath four times in a row. Explain that this takes longer and may require more focus. For the first attempt, guide them with your words: **Now, let's do 4 × 4 × 4 breathing. That's when we do this in-and-out breathing four times in a row. Remember to begin with blowing out. Count to four each time you exhale and inhale. Ready? Exhale . . . inhale . . . exhale . . . inhale . . . exhale . . . inhale . . . exhale . . . inhale.**

Wrap-Up

Remind students: **Your breath is a valuable tool that is with you all the time. It has been used for thousands of years to calm the body and mind.**

Explain: **The 4 × 4 breathing cycle is a kind of reset button for the mind and body. When you are feeling upset, doing the simple 4 × 4 breath can calm down your body. But just doing this once may not give your thoughts and feelings enough time to calm down. Just like the glitter in the jar from earlier, your body needs time to settle. Going through four breath cycles—4 × 4 × 4 breathing—usually gives you the right amount of time for feelings to settle.**

Mindful Checkout

Invite students to find a comfortable position and sit quietly. Choose one of these activities to guide your students through a mindful checkout, referencing "Mindful Pauses to Begin and End Lessons" on page 17 for guidance as needed:

- Practice Breath Awareness
- Be Mindful of Change
- Practice the first two steps of the Pause (STOP and 4 × 4 × 4 breathing)

Follow-Up

Throughout the day, you may want to pause and ask students to practice 4 × 4 × 4 breathing. Over time, this mindful breathing can become a kind of calming reflex that students use instinctively when they start to become upset.

Variation
4 × 4 Breathing with Holding Breath

Try this after students have learned the basic 4 × 4 breathing. Add holding the breath for a count of four after the exhalation. The 4 × 4 breathing variation with holding breath goes like this:

1. Exhale to a count of four.

2. Hold your breath to a count of four.

3. Inhale to a count of four.

This practice can lead to increased calm and breath awareness. *Note: Don't try this variation right after kids have been doing a lot of physical activity, because it involves holding their breath briefly.*

STOP ("PAUSE" STEP 1)

S—Stop:
Stop what you are doing.

T—Take a Breath:
Take a deep belly breath.

O—Observe:
Notice what is happening inside and outside of you.

P—Proceed:
Think and decide on the best action to take next.

Name:_____ Date:_____

From *Teaching Kids to Pause, Cope, and Connect: Lessons for Social-Emotional Learning and Mindfulness* by Mark Purcell, Psy.D., and Kellen Glinder, M.D., copyright © 2022. This page may be reproduced for individual, classroom, or small group work only. For other uses, contact Free Spirit Publishing at freespirit.com/permissions.

TAKE A BREATH:
4 × 4 BREATHING ("PAUSE" STEP 2)

1... 2...
3... 4...

1... 2...
3... 4...

4   **×**   **4**

Name:_____ Date:_____

From *Teaching Kids to Pause, Cope, and Connect: Lessons for Social-Emotional Learning and Mindfulness* by Mark Purcell, Psy.D., and Kellen Glinder, M.D., copyright © 2022. This page may be reproduced for individual, classroom, or small group work only. For other uses, contact Free Spirit Publishing at freespirit.com/permissions.

TAKE A BREATH: 4 × 4 × 4 BREATHING

1

4   ×   4

2

4   ×   4

3

4   ×   4

4

4   ×   4

Name:_____ Date:_____

From *Teaching Kids to Pause, Cope, and Connect: Lessons for Social-Emotional Learning and Mindfulness* by Mark Purcell, Psy.D., and Kellen Glinder, M.D., copyright © 2022. This page may be reproduced for individual, classroom, or small group work only. For other uses, contact Free Spirit Publishing at freespirit.com/permissions.

LESSON 8
MINDFUL DETECTIVE (COPE)

Lesson Summary

In this lesson, students will practice one of the primary skills of mindfulness: to observe and describe experiences.

Keywords

- thoughts
- feelings
- body signals
- noticing
- describing
- investigating feelings
- Mindful Detective

Students Will

- identify the difference between thoughts, feelings, and body signals
- learn how these systems communicate with each other

Materials

- "Mindful Detective" handout

Preparation

On the whiteboard, copy the diagram from the "Mindful Detective" handout. Write the word *Thoughts* with a thought bubble next to it, the word *Feelings* with a heart next to it, and the phrase *Body Signals* with the outline of a body next to it.

Mindful Check-In

Invite students to find a comfortable position and close their eyes or gently gaze downward. Guide them through the first two steps of the Pause (STOP and 4 × 4 × 4 breathing) for a mindful check-in. Reference the preceding lesson or "Mindful Pauses to Begin and End Lessons" on page 17 as needed.

Activity

Refer students to the whiteboard where *Thoughts*, *Feelings*, and *Body Signals* are written next to their corresponding images.

1. Point to the thought bubble and ask: **What are thoughts?** Elicit some answers from students. Explain: **Thoughts are the statements we say inside of our minds.** Ask for some examples of thoughts. Give a few examples if students do not come up with any. Ask: **Are thoughts always true?** Briefly discuss how our thoughts are the ways we look at things, and this can change.

2. Point to the heart and ask: **What are feelings?** Elicit answers from students like *mad*, *sad*, *scared*, and *happy*. Explain that feelings are also called emotions. Say: **Emotions are what we feel in our hearts in a situation.** Point to the image of the heart. **But we may feel them in more places**

than our hearts. Discuss further, knowing that it can be hard to describe where feelings come from.

3. Point at the outline of the body and ask: **What is a signal?** Elicit answers like *a sign, a message,* or *a clue that tells us something.* A good example is a traffic light that signals go, wait, stop. **What are some of the signals our body sends to our brain?** Elicit answers like *feeling hot/cold, feeling tired,* and *muscle aches.*

4. Explain: **We are going to be learning more about thoughts, feelings, and body signals during the coming lessons. Right now, let's play a fun game to learn to notice which of these things is happening inside of us.**

Noticing Thoughts, Feelings, and Body Signals Activity

1. Ask students to stand up and spread out far enough that they can't touch each other with their arms outstretched.

2. Say: **I am going to make a statement, and I want each of you to let me know if it is a *thought*, a *feeling*, or a *body signal*.**

3. Say: **If what I say is a *thought*, place your hand on your head.** Demonstrate.

4. Say: **If what I say is a *feeling*, place your hand on your heart.** Demonstrate.

5. Say: **If what I say is a *body signal*, wiggle your hands and arms at your sides.** Demonstrate.

6. Call out examples of each while students do the action that represents what the statement is.

   a. For *thoughts*, use statements and opinions. Examples: "I am lazy," "My brother is mean," "PE is the best class."

   b. For *feelings*, identify specific emotions. Examples: "I'm sad because I lost the game," "I'm mad because we got homework," "I'm happy because it's my birthday."

   c. For *body signals,* name specific physical sensations. Examples: "My stomach hurts," "I'm tired," "I have a headache."

7. Play this game for two to three minutes, then ask students to stand still.

8. Say: **In real life, we don't have people calling these things out. We have to use our inner detective to notice what we're thinking, what emotions we're feeling, and what we're feeling in our bodies.**

9. Make sure students have about three to five feet of space around them.

10. Explain: **If you are comfortable with it, I am going to ask you to close your eyes. If you aren't comfortable closing your eyes, try to look downward, toward the floor. With eyes closed or looking down, I want you to slowly explore the space around you without moving your feet. You can move the rest of your body, but please keep your feet in place so you don't bump into other students.**

11. Say: **I want you to turn your attention inward while you do this. I'll ask questions while you're exploring to help you do that.**

12. Instruct students to begin exploring with their eyes closed or cast downward.

13. Ask: **What kinds of signals is your body giving you? Notice and answer silently in your mind.** Allow students thirty seconds to observe their body signals.

14. Ask: **What kinds of thoughts are you having? Notice and answer silently to yourself.** Allow students thirty seconds to observe their thoughts.

15. Ask: **What kinds of feelings are you having? Notice and answer in your mind.** Allow students thirty seconds to observe their feelings.

16. When students have finished the activity, have them open their eyes and take their seats.

Direct students' attention to the diagram on the whiteboard and the words written there: *Thoughts*, *Feelings*, and *Body Signals*. Ask students to share some of each type that came up during the activity. Write them down on the whiteboard in the corresponding area.

Ask: **Did signals from your body affect what you thought? Did they affect how you felt?** Say: **For example, did you feel nervous about having your eyes closed? Did that cause you to think about what others were doing?** Elicit examples or ask for suggestions based on some of the body signals written on the board. Then draw dotted lines between "Body Signals" and the other two areas.

Ask: **How about your thoughts? Did what you were thinking affect your feelings? Did your thoughts affect the signals you were getting from your body?** Say: **For example, if you were thinking about playing with your friends after school, what feelings did you have? What body signals changed?** Elicit examples or ask for suggestions using examples from the list on the board. Draw dotted lines between "Thoughts" and the other two areas.

Ask: **Lastly, did your emotions change your body signals? Did they change your thoughts?** Say: **For example, if you felt excited, you might have felt your heart race or your muscles tense. Or if you felt joyful, you might have thought, "This is fun!"** Elicit examples or ask for suggestions based on the feelings written on the board. Draw dotted lines from "Feelings" to the other two areas.

Direct students' attention to the three areas on the board: thoughts, feelings, and body signals. Explain: **These three areas talk to each other. When one changes, the others change. When you closed your eyes, the signals from your body to your heart and mind changed. Then those parts of you spoke to each other and back to your body. We don't notice it most of the time, but there is a *conversation* happening inside of us all the time. A conversation is when people talk to each other. But this conversation is between our thoughts, feelings, and body.**

Wrap-Up

In the upper left corner of the whiteboard, draw an eye. Then draw dotted lines showing the eye watching over the diagram of thoughts, feelings, and body signals.

Explain: **Mindfulness is about learning to watch this conversation inside of us, to simply notice what we are thinking, what we are feeling, and what signals our body is sending. We can call that being a Mindful Detective.**

Draw a magnifying glass in front of the watchful eye.

Direct students to the "Mindful Detective" handout. Explain: **You have now learned the third part of the Pause: Mindful Detective. After you STOP and take your 4 × 4 breaths, finish these three sentences:**

- "In my body, I feel . . ."
- "I am thinking . . ."
- "I am feeling . . ."

Explain: **If we are aware of these thoughts, feelings, and body signals, then we can make better decisions about what to *do*. We will learn about that part of the Pause next week.**

Mindful Checkout

Invite students to find a comfortable position and sit quietly. Choose one of these activities to guide your students through a mindful checkout, referencing "Mindful Pauses to Begin and End Lessons" on page 17 for guidance as needed:

- Practice Breath Awareness
- Be Mindful of Change
- Practice the first three steps of the Pause (STOP, 4 × 4 × 4 breathing, and Mindful Detective)

Follow-Up

Throughout the following week, take breaks and practice the first three steps of the Pause. Instruct students to practice STOP, and then do some 4 × 4 × 4 breathing. Next, guide them through noticing what signals they are getting from their bodies (pause to allow them time to observe); then what they are feeling (pause); and lastly, what they are thinking (pause).

MINDFUL DETECTIVE ("PAUSE" STEP 3)

Thoughts

Body Signals

Feelings

Name:_____ Date:_____

From *Teaching Kids to Pause, Cope, and Connect: Lessons for Social-Emotional Learning and Mindfulness* by Mark Purcell, Psy.D., and Kellen Glinder, M.D., copyright © 2022. This page may be reproduced for individual, classroom, or small group work only. For other uses, contact Free Spirit Publishing at freespirit.com/permissions.

LESSON 9
WISE ACTION (CONNECT)

Lesson Summary

Students learn the final step of the Pause: choosing Wise Action.

Keywords

- thoughts
- feelings
- body signals
- Mindful Detective
- Wise Actions

Students Will

- learn how our thoughts, feelings, and body signals inform the actions we take
- understand the Wise Action process

Materials

- "Wise Action" handout
- "The Pause" handout
- "Wise Action Scenes" teacher resource
- *optional*: a bell

Preparation

- One the whiteboard, copy the "Mindful Detective" diagram from the previous lesson (see "Mindful Detective" handout). This time, include a section on the left side that reads "Something Happens" and a section on the right side that reads "Action/What We Do." This is the Wise Action diagram. For an example of how this might look, see the "Wise Action" student handout on page 68.

Mindful Check-In

Invite students to find a comfortable position and close their eyes or look downward. Guide them through the first three steps of the Pause (STOP, 4 × 4 × 4 breathing, and Mindful Detective) for a mindful check-in. Reference the preceding lesson or "Mindful Pauses to Begin and End Lessons" on page 17 as needed.

Activity

Begin by referencing the diagram on the whiteboard showing the three areas: thoughts, feelings, and body signals. Say: **Remember when we discussed how these three parts talk to each other from inside our head, heart, and body? Now, we're going to learn how their conversations tell us what to do.** If needed, remind students that conversations are when people—or parts of the body—talk to each other. Let students know that they are going to do a mini play to learn how this happens.

The Conversation Inside Me (Part 1)

1. Pick one of the skits from the "Wise Action Scenes" teacher resource. Say: **We're going to do a mini play. For this mini play, we'll need a total of five actors. Two people will play the characters. Three people will play the main character's thoughts, feelings, and body signals. Those three are going to act out the conversation inside the main character.**

2. Ask for two students to play the characters, identified here as "Student A" and "Student B." The two will act out a scene, and Student A (the main character) will have to make a decision partway through.

3. Ask for three more volunteers. Have each play one of these three parts:
   - The Brain (Thoughts)
   - The Heart (Feelings)
   - The Body (Body Signals)

4. Tell the students playing Brain, Heart, and Body that each of them must try to convince Student A to listen to them.

5. Explain that you will ring the bell (or clap) to begin the mini play. The students will have a limited amount of time to act it out (two to three minutes). Tell them that when you clap the second time, the scene will end, and Student A will have to decide *what to do.*

6. Read the Wise Action scene aloud to the students.

7. Ring the bell, or clap your hands, and say "Action!"

8. Let the actors act out the scene for a few moments until the dramatic event happens to Student A.

9. Ask the other three actors to start trying to persuade Student A to listen to them and to argue with each other over what action the main character should take, all speaking at the same time.

10. Allow this to become somewhat chaotic with everyone talking at once until Student A can barely understand what is being said.

11. Ring the bell (or clap your hands) and tell Student A: **You need to decide what to do *right now*!**

12. After Student A makes a decision, have Student A and Student B act that decision out. Then, ring the bell and say "Cut!" to end the scene.

13. On the board, write down the initial dramatic event under the label "Something Happens." Then you can write what Student A decided to do under the label "Action/What We Do."

14. Ask Student A to share what it was like trying to make a decision with all that noise.

15. Explain: **In upsetting situations, this is often what is happening inside us, and we don't even know it. Our thoughts, feelings, and bodies are yelling back and forth. We don't pause to listen. Then we might end up acting in a way that isn't good for ourselves or others.**

The Conversation Inside Me (Part 2)

1. Assemble the same group of actors. Say "Action!" to start the scene.

2. This time, when the dramatic event occurs, ring the bell (or clap your hands) and say "Pause."

3. Ask all the actors to stop talking. Then invite them to take some 4 × 4 breaths.

4. Tell Student A: **Now you can slow things down and talk to each part of you. You can ask the Brain what it's thinking. Then ask the Heart what it's feeling. And ask the Body what signals it's sending.**

5. Ask the different parts—Brain, Heart, and Body—to describe what they might be experiencing. Encourage a dialogue between Student A and each part.

6. Allow Student A some time to talk to each character.

7. After Student A seems done talking, you can ring the bell or clap. Then ask Student A, "What is the Wise Action to take?"

8. Wait for Student A's answer, then allow Student A and Student B to act that decision out and finish the scene.

Discuss: **What was different about the two scenes? How did the Pause help the main character make a wise decision?**

Direct students' attention to the full Wise Action diagram on the whiteboard. Walk them through the process they just witnessed or acted out. Name the event that occurred in the skit (Something Happens). Next, point out the three parts

that talked to each other (Brain, Heart, and Body). Then point to the response (What We Do). Identify that as the Wise Action.

If time permits, ask for five more volunteers and pick a different scene to act out. For this second scene, go through both Part 1 and Part 2 again.

Explain: **This is the final step of the Pause. I know this can seem kind of hard or complicated now. But we will have lots of chances to keep practicing this.**

Direct students to their "The Pause" handout, or write the four steps on the whiteboard. Lead the class through the four steps of the Pause:

1. STOP: Stop, Take a Breath, Observe, Proceed

2. 4 × 4 × 4 breathing

3. Mindful Detective: Ask the three questions below.

   a. *What do I feel in my body?*

   b. *What do I feel in my heart?*

   c. *What am I thinking?*

4. Take Wise Action: If an action is needed, this is the time to take it.

Wrap-Up

Explain: **You can practice the Pause anywhere and anytime. It will take lots of practice to get used to it. It's best to start by using it when you feel calm. Then, with practice, you will be able to use the Pause during upsetting situations. And if you can learn to pause before you act, you may be able to stop yourself from doing things that create problems for you and others. Think of**

it as pressing the Pause button. When you start again, you will be in control of what you do.

Mindful Checkout

Invite students to find a comfortable position and sit quietly. Choose one of these activities to guide your students through a mindful checkout, referencing "Mindful Pauses to Begin and End Lessons" on page 17 for guidance as needed:

- Practice Breath Awareness
- Be Mindful of Change
- Practice the Pause

Follow-Up

During the next week, try to practice the Pause every day so that students can remember the steps. For the rest of the lessons in this book, practice the Pause during the mindful check-in and, if desired, during the mindful checkout. Students may not always need to decide on a Wise Action, but they can do the first three steps of the Pause at any time.

Considerations

Be mindful of students with sensory concerns, particularly sensitivity to sound, while the students perform the mini play. The actors shouting and talking over each other may be overwhelming. Give these students the option to wear headphones or leave the room during the play. If a student who is sensitive to sound is acting in the mini play, explain what they should expect and allow them to cover their ears if needed.

WISE ACTION ("PAUSE" STEP 4)

Thoughts

Something Happens

Action: What We Do

Body Signals

Feelings

Name:_____ Date:_____

From *Teaching Kids to Pause, Cope, and Connect: Lessons for Social-Emotional Learning and Mindfulness* by Mark Purcell, Psy.D., and Kellen Glinder, M.D., copyright © 2022. This page may be reproduced for individual, classroom, or small group work only. For other uses, contact Free Spirit Publishing at freespirit.com/permissions.

THE PAUSE

Follow the steps below to complete The Pause:

STOP

S— Stop: Stop what you are doing.

T— Take a Breath: Take a mindful belly breath.

O— Observe: Notice what is happening inside and outside of you.

P— Proceed: Think and decide the best action to take next.

1

4 × 4

2

4 × 4

3

4 × 4

4 × 4 × 4 Breathing - - - - - - - → **4**

4 × 4

Mindful Detective - - - - - - - - - →

Thoughts

Body Signals

Feelings

Observe your **thoughts**, **feelings**, and **body signals**.

Fill in these statements:

I am thinking ____,

The emotions I am feeling are ____.

In my body, I am feeling ____,

Wise Action - - - - - - - →

Thoughts

Something Happens

Action: What We Do

Body Signals

Feelings

What is the best action to take?

Name:_____ Date:_____

From *Teaching Kids to Pause, Cope, and Connect: Lessons for Social-Emotional Learning and Mindfulness* by Mark Purcell, Psy.D., and Kellen Glinder, M.D., copyright © 2022. This page may be reproduced for individual, classroom, or small group work only. For other uses, contact Free Spirit Publishing at freespirit.com/permissions.

WISE ACTION SCENES

Use the scenes below to act out the skits for the Wise Action activity.

1. My Turn!

Keenan and Miguel are playing video games at Keenan's house. They are playing a single-player game and are supposed to take turns. Keenan has a long turn, then finally goofs up and his turn ends. But instead of giving Miguel a chance to play, he says, "Let me go again; I almost made it." Then he restarts the game.

What does Miguel . . .

    a. *Feel/sense in his body?*

    b. *Feel in his heart?*

    c. *Think?*

2. Foul!

At recess, Tran is playing freeze tag while Travis plays basketball. Travis takes a long shot and the rebound hits Tran when she's not looking.

What does Tran . . .

    a. *Feel/sense in her body?*

    b. *Feel in her heart?*

    c. *Think?*

3. Disaster Project

Aliyah and Nia are working together on a science project that has taken them all week. Aliyah rushes through the experiment, and the materials spill everywhere. Their project is ruined.

What does Nia. . .

    a. *Feel/sense in her body?*

    b. *Feel in her heart?*

    c. *Think?*

From *Teaching Kids to Pause, Cope, and Connect: Lessons for Social-Emotional Learning and Mindfulness* by Mark Purcell, Psy.D., and Kellen Glinder, M.D., copyright © 2022. This page may be reproduced for individual, classroom, or small group work only. For other uses, contact Free Spirit Publishing at freespirit.com/permissions.

LIFE SKILL IV
NOTICE BODY SIGNALS

In many cases, our bodies react to stress before we have time to realize it. We can feel tense immediately when surprised, yet the realization of what has happened washes over us much later. The same can be true with low-level chronic stress. Our shoulders may be tense, our brows may be furrowed, and our heart rates and breathing rates may elevate.

These bodily functions make our brains more alert and more vigilant in the moment. That's important and helpful. However, when a person experiences persistent increases in tension, chronic stress can result. The body and the brain are connected in such a way that stress signals from one affect the other. Conversely, learning to calm one can help calm the other. The lessons in this section are designed to introduce the concept of this mind-body connection to students and begin their process of noticing how calming the body can help calm the mind and vice versa.

Introducing This Life Skill to Students

There are various options for introducing the Notice Body Signals life skill based on the needs of your group and your time limitations. The following lessons provide different learning experiences related to the Notice Body Signals life skill. If you are limited on time, you can start with the first lesson. Otherwise, you can introduce the skill with quotations and class discussion or by reading related books.

1. **Quotations and Socratic Questioning:** You may start a brief discussion by reading one of the quotations listed below (or another one chosen by you).

   • "Our bodies communicate to us clearly and specifically, if we are willing to listen." —Shakti Gawain

- "The mind's first step to self-awareness must be through the body."
  —George Sheehan

Follow up your chosen quotation with questions such as:

- What does this quote mean to you?
- How does it relate to the life skill of Notice Body Signals or body awareness?
- Why do you think it is important to notice what we are feeling in our bodies?
- Can you share a time when you noticed your body's signals?

2. **Related Literature:** You may wish to connect this life skill to relevant children's literature. You can begin a lesson by reading one of the books listed below, or you can read parts of it between the three lessons related to this life skill.

- *I Am a Feeling Body: Body Awareness and Mindfulness for Children* by Douglas Macauley
- *My Magic Breath: Finding Calm Through Mindful Breathing* by Nick Ortner and Alison Taylor
- *My Incredible Talking Body: Learning to Be Calm* by Rebecca Bowen

Further Resources

- "What Is the 'Mind-Body Connection'?" by Mightier, mightier.com/articles/emotional-regulation/what-is-the-mind-body-connection
- "4 Ways to Develop Mind-Body Awareness with Young Children" by Emily Gold, activeforlife.com/mind-body-awareness-children
- "Teaching Kids the Mind Body Connection: When Anxiety Physically Hurts" and video "Learn How Anxiety Can Make You Sick (and What to Do About It)" by Natasha Daniels, anxioustoddlers.com/teaching-kids-the-mind-body-connection

LESSON 10
BODY SCAN AND TRACE (PAUSE)

Lesson Summary

In this activity, students will learn how to do a body scan, which is an important mindfulness practice. Then they will draw the sensations they felt on a body outline.

Keywords

- body sensations
- body scan

Students Will

- learn how to do a body scan
- develop more body awareness

Materials

- crayons, colored pencils, or markers
- "Body Trace" handout

Mindful Check-In

Guide students through the Pause for a mindful check-in, referencing "Mindful Pauses to Begin and End Lessons" on page 17 for guidance as needed.

Activity

Invite students to get into a comfortable seated position with their hands on their laps.

Explain: **A very useful part of mindfulness is learning how to listen to our bodies. Our bodies can tell us a lot about how we are doing and what we are feeling.** Review the five senses (sight, smell, hearing, taste, and touch) and what we mean by the word *sensations*. Elicit a few examples of sensations from students.

Describe: **For this activity, we are going to focus our attention inward and slowly scan our bodies from our toes all the way up to the tops of our heads. To scan means to examine. As we go through the body scan, just notice what you feel in each part of your body. If you find that it's hard to focus, that's normal. Gently practice coming back again and again to what you are feeling in your body.**

Body Scan

Use the script below to guide students through a body scan. Pause momentarily between paragraphs for students to follow the instructions and consider what they feel. You can adjust this script as needed for time constraints or student needs.

This body scan script is adapted from "Body Scan for Kids" in "Mindfulness Meditation: Guided Practices" by Mark Bertin, originally published at mindful .org/mindfulness-meditation-guided -practices. Reprinted with permission.

Say: **Lie down on your back** (or, if you are doing the worksheet body trace, say: **Sit up straight in your chair**). Let your legs relax, and let your arms relax and fall to the sides. Settle yourself in a comfortable position. If you like, you can close your eyes or gaze downward. For these few minutes, let yourself be still. There's nothing to do. Pay attention as best you can.

Start by taking two or three big, gentle breaths. Pay attention to how that feels. Your belly rises and falls. Air moves in and out of your body. If you like, place a hand on your belly and feel it move with each breath.

Now we're going to pay attention to the other parts of the body. Start with your feet. They might feel warm or cold, wet or dry, relaxed or restless. It's also okay if you feel nothing at all. If you can, relax your feet now. If that's hard to do, that's fine. Take a moment and notice how that feels too. You might feel socks or shoes on your feet, or you might feel your feet pressing against the floor. When your mind gets busy, gently bring your attention back to your feet again.

Now, move your attention to your lower legs, noticing whatever is there. Do they feel heavy, light, warm, cold, or something else? Let go of frustration and trying to do anything. Just do your best and give yourself a few moments of rest.

Next, move your attention to your knees and relax them. Notice any sensations on the front, back, and sides of your knees.

After a few more breaths, move your attention to your upper legs. Whatever you feel, or don't feel, is fine. Notice your legs and let them relax. If you feel restless or wiggly, that's okay too. That happens.

Now move your attention to your belly. It always moves when you breathe, rising and falling, like waves on the sea. You might feel something on the inside, like full or hungry. You might even feel emotions in your belly, like happy or sad or upset.

Next, bring your attention to your chest. Notice it rising and falling as you breathe. If you feel that it's hard to focus, that's okay. Gently practice coming back again and again to how your chest feels when you breathe.

Now, turn your attention to your hands. There is no need to move them or do anything with them. They may be touching the floor or resting on your body. Relax them if you can, and if not, simply pay attention to your hands for another moment.

Move your attention up into your arms. Maybe notice if you can find a moment of stillness inside you, like the pause at the end of each breath.

Next, move your attention around to your back. How does it feel against the chair? Notice how it rocks with each breath. When your mind gets busy or angry or scared, you can always come back to how your body feels in this way for a moment.

Now move your attention to your neck and shoulders, letting go and relaxing them. If your mind wanders, that's fine. No one can pay attention all the time. Just keep returning to noticing your body whenever you find yourself thinking of something else.

And now notice how your face and head feel. What expression do you have on your face right now? What would it feel like to smile? What else do you notice in your face, in your head, and in your mind?

Finally, spend a few moments paying attention to your whole body. If it is easier, continue to pay attention to your breath. When you are ready, open your eyes and be still for a few moments before moving again.

Ask students to briefly share how they felt doing the body scan.

Body Trace

1. Ask students to use the coloring supplies to draw what they felt in the different parts of their bodies in the outline on the "Body Trace" handout.

2. If students get stuck, you can provide some examples, like red flames in spots where they felt warm, blue where they felt cold, or little spikes where they may have felt prickly sensations.

3. Ask for a few volunteers to share their drawings, encouraging them to describe the different sensations they felt in their bodies.

Wrap-Up

Explain to students that the body scan is a very important part of mindfulness because our bodies can often give us signals about how we are doing. Give a few examples of this, or elicit examples from students. For instance, you could say: **When you are stressed out, you may feel tightness in your neck and shoulders. Or when you are nervous, you might feel a twisty feeling in your tummy.**

Explain: **Learning to listen to our bodies can help us know what's happening inside of us. This can tell us what we may need to do to feel better or calmer. The body scan can also be a great tool to help you relax and get ready for sleep. If you have trouble turning off your brain and falling asleep at night, try to practice the body scan.**

Mindful Checkout

Invite students to find a comfortable position and sit quietly. Choose one of these activities to guide your students through a mindful checkout, referencing "Mindful Pauses to Begin and End Lessons" on page 17 for guidance as needed:

- Practice the Pause
- Be Mindful of Change

Follow-Up

During the following week, you may want to take brief pauses and have students do a mini body scan, which can be done in a minute or two. Have them sit still and take 4 × 4 × 4 breaths to focus. Then, have them scan their bodies, starting at their feet and moving up to their heads, and just notice what sensations they feel.

Guide them through the scan as needed. If many of your students can do this independently, then just focus on any students needing some extra help. If students are struggling with concentrating on the 4 × 4 × 4 breathing and mini body scan on their own, continue with guided body scans and offer additional support and direction if needed.

Considerations

In this activity, concerns around body image or physical limitations may arise. Remind students of their community commitments and to treat each other with respect and kindness before beginning the activity.

BODY TRACE

In the body outline, draw the different sensations you felt while doing the body scan.

Name:_____ Date:_____

From *Teaching Kids to Pause, Cope, and Connect: Lessons for Social-Emotional Learning and Mindfulness* by Mark Purcell, Psy.D., and Kellen Glinder, M.D., copyright © 2022. This page may be reproduced for individual, classroom, or small group work only. For other uses, contact Free Spirit Publishing at freespirit.com/permissions.

LESSON 11
YOUR STRESS METER (COPE)

Lesson Summary

This activity builds on the body scan by having students use body awareness to alert them when emotions are becoming too intense.

Keywords

- coping skills
- stress
- stress meter

Students Will

- use a thermometer-shaped stress meter to rank their stress and tension on a scale of 1 to 10
- identify the body signals related to different levels of stress and tension

Materials

- "My Stress Meter" handout

Mindful Check-In

Guide students through the Pause for a mindful check-in, referencing "Mindful Pauses to Begin and End Lessons" on page 17 for guidance as needed.

Activity

Explain: **Grown-ups might tell you things you can do when you start to get upset, like taking deep breaths,** listening to music, or doing something alone in your room. We sometimes call these activities *coping skills* because they can help us cope, or deal with, upsetting feelings. But often, these coping skills don't work. Does anyone know why?

Take a few moments to elicit answers from students.

Answer: **The reason these don't always work is that sometimes we are *too* upset. Our feelings have gotten too strong for the coping skills to calm us down.**

Explain: **In the last lesson, we learned how to listen to our bodies for signals about how we are feeling. You can use that same awareness to notice when your feelings are getting too big to manage.**

Refer students to the "My Stress Meter" handout.

1. Draw a thermometer similar to the one on the handout on the whiteboard. At the top, write "Stress Meter."
2. Write the numbers 0–10 in the thermometer.
3. On the top of the left side, write "Feelings."
4. On the top of the right side, write "Body Signals" and, below that, "How It Feels in My Body."

5. Ask: **What does the word *stress* mean?** Elicit a few answers. Explain: **Stress is when our minds, feelings, or bodies are pushed too hard by things happening around us. Stress can start small and build up, sometimes slowly, other times very quickly, until we can't control it.**

6. On the board, pick a general feeling to write in all caps beneath "Feelings." Possible feelings include *angry*, *sad*, *happy*, or *afraid*.

7. Explain: **As we've been talking about, feelings can sometimes get so big inside us that we can't control them. But if we learn to listen closely to our bodies, we can get signals that our feelings are becoming too strong. The sooner we notice, the easier it is to use a coping skill to keep the feeling from getting too big to handle.**

8. Walk students through the process of filling out a stress meter. Starting from the bottom of the stress meter, write degrees of the general feeling you picked on the left. Write corresponding physical sensations on the right. As you move up the scale, write down emotions of increasing intensity and related physical sensations. You can copy the example below or create your own.

> Example Feeling: Anger
>
> Related Feelings: 1—calm; 3—irritated; 5—mad; 7—furious; 10—enraged
>
> How It Feels in My Body: 1—relaxed muscles; 3—tense muscles; 5—heart beating faster; 7—body feeling hot, 10—muscles tensing all over

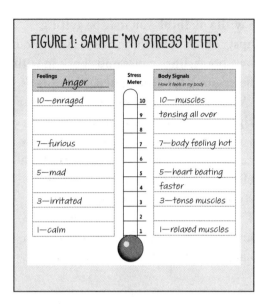

FIGURE 1: SAMPLE 'MY STRESS METER'

Feelings Anger	Stress Meter	Body Signals How it feels in my body
10—enraged	10	10—muscles tensing all over
	9	
	8	
7—furious	7	7—body feeling hot
	6	
5—mad	5	5—heart beating faster
	4	
3—irritated	3	3—tense muscles
	2	
1—calm	1	1—relaxed muscles

9. After you finish, instruct students to fill out their own stress meters.

10. Explain: **Each of you may have a different feeling that gets out of control for you. For some of you, it may be feeing angry; for others, it may be feeling afraid. Even feeling happy can get out of control.**

11. Say: **Pick your feeling and write it at the top.** Review the instructions on the handout. Then say: **If you can think of the different levels of this feeling you experience, write them on the left side. If you can't think of other words for the feeling, that's okay. You can leave some spaces blank.**

12. When students have finished, congratulate them on completing their stress meters. Ask for a few volunteers to share their stress meters.

Wrap-Up

Discuss with students how listening to their bodies can be a way of knowing when they are starting to get upset.

Say: **If you think you may be getting upset about something or overwhelmed by a big feeling, pause and check in with how your body feels. Then ask yourself, "What number am I on my stress meter right now?" The earlier you realize your feelings are getting too strong, the earlier you can choose to do something else, like a coping skill, to keep your stress meter from shooting up higher. This is important because, as we all know, when we reach 9 or 10, it's much harder to control what we do or say.**

Mindful Checkout

Invite students to find a comfortable position and sit quietly. Choose one of these activities to guide your students through a mindful checkout, referencing "Mindful Pauses to Begin and End Lessons" on page 17 for guidance as needed:

- Practice the Pause
- Be Mindful of Change

Follow-Up

Make extra copies of the "My Stress Meter" handout and keep them available for students to pick up and use when they want or need to. When you notice that a student may be starting to get upset about something, ask them what number they are on their stress meter. You can also ask them to identify what they are feeling and how strong the feeling is from 0 to 10. Follow up by asking if there is something they can do (or you can help them with) to bring the number down. You can also encourage students to take their stress meters home and share them with their families.

Variations
Drawing the Stress Meter

You can have students draw out how their body feels at different levels instead of writing out the sensations. For example, squiggly lines around hands can show shakiness. This is a good option for younger students without the vocabulary to identify different emotions or physical reactions.

Include Behaviors

Next to the column "Feelings" on the stress meter, you can also add a "What I Do" column. Ask students to include what actions they tend to take at the different levels of the stress meter. Explain that, just like body signals, noticing what you do when you have an upset feeling can help you know that you may need to pause or ask for help.

MY STRESS METER

1. Think of a feeling that sometimes becomes too big for you, like anger, fear, or sadness. Write it on the line under the word "Feelings" on the top left side of the thermometer.

2. In the spaces under your feeling, list the levels of the feeling that build up next to the numbers that show how strong the feeling is. For example, if your main feeling is fear, you could write the word *calm* at the bottom next to the number 1. Then, go up the scale adding other words next to the numbers from 2 to 10. Some ideas might be *uneasy, anxious, worried, stressed, afraid, scared, frightened,* and *terrified*. It's okay not to fill in all of the spaces.

3. On the right side under "Body Signals," write down how each level of the feeling feels inside your body.

Feelings	Stress Meter	Body Signals *How it feels in my body*
	10	
	9	
	8	
	7	
	6	
	5	
	4	
	3	
	2	
	1	

Name:_____ Date:_____

From *Teaching Kids to Pause, Cope, and Connect: Lessons for Social-Emotional Learning and Mindfulness* by Mark Purcell, Psy.D., and Kellen Glinder, M.D., copyright © 2022. This page may be reproduced for individual, classroom, or small group work only. For other uses, contact Free Spirit Publishing at freespirit.com/permissions.

LESSON 12
ADJUST YOUR FEELINGS' VOLUME (CONNECT)

Lesson Summary

In this lesson, students will build upon the understanding of emotional scales that they developed in Lesson 11: Your Stress Meter. They will learn to identify when the "volume" (intensity) of their feelings doesn't match the situation.

Note: Often, students are told by adults that they "shouldn't be so mad" or sad or upset. That can feel invalidating for children because they often have a good reason for how they are feeling. Problems often come from the intensity of those feelings and how they are expressed in the situation. Rather than invalidating the child's emotional response, teachers can validate the feeling while guiding the child in adjusting the intensity and expression of that feeling. The skill of adjusting the "volume" (intensity) of the feeling—instead of shutting it off entirely—can be useful for both teachers and students. Teachers can use it to help students regulate their emotions while still validating them. And students can use it to learn to accept how they feel while gaining some self-control.

Keywords

- feelings
- volume

Students Will

- learn that all feelings are acceptable
- learn how to communicate feelings to teachers, parents, and others
- realize that the intensity of feelings may not always match the situation
- reflect on situations when their feelings' intensity was stronger than needed
- practice adjusting their feelings' "volume"

Materials

- "Feeling Too Loud" handout
- "My Stress Meter" handout
- "Adjust Your Feelings' Volume" handout
- cell phone or other device to play music for the class

Mindful Check-In

Guide students through the Pause for a mindful check-in, referencing "Mindful Pauses to Begin and End Lessons" on page 17 for guidance as needed.

Activity

Have the students stand. Play music that is somewhat loud and jarring, like heavy metal or techno. In a soft voice, instruct

the students to get into their seats as you turn the volume up until students cannot hear you over the loud music. Then dial the volume down until it is playing softly in the background (at this point you may even switch the music to a genre that is more soothing).

Ask students whether it was difficult for them to hear what you were saying. Ask: **How did you feel in your body when the music was loud?**

Explain: **Just like that loud music, our feelings can become so loud inside us that we can barely hear our own thoughts. It can help to learn how to turn down our feelings' "volume" so we can think more clearly. Turning down the volume on our feelings can also help us tell others how we feel or what we need.**

Feeling Too Loud

1. Ask for two volunteers and have them read one of the scenarios from the "Feeling Too Loud" handout to themselves.

2. Have the volunteers pick which character they want to play, or assign them roles. Give the actors a few moments to imagine the skit and how they want to act it out.

3. During that time, privately instruct one of them to exaggerate how upset they are.

4. Have the students act out the scene for about three minutes. When they finish, ask the group to rate the upset actor's stress meter level from 1 to 10 using the "My Stress Meter" handout. Ask them to name the feeling the upset actor expressed.

5. Ask: **Do you think this situation called for level _____ (number rating students gave) _____ (feeling students named)?** For example, you might ask, "Do you think this situation called for level 8 fear?" Ask: **What do you think might be a more appropriate feeling level for this kind of situation?**

6. Ask the student audience what else they noticed during the exchange. They may have noticed that the student who was not instructed to exaggerate their feelings became louder and more argumentative during the interaction. Discuss why that might have happened.

7. Have the students reverse roles and act the scenario out again. This time, instruct the students to express their feelings at a level that matches the situation. If students argue or feel that some more intense feelings are justified, explain that the point is to show that when feelings are expressed more calmly, the volume and stress can go lower.

Adjust Your Feelings' Volume

Divide students into pairs. Instruct them to complete the "Adjust Your Feelings' Volume" handout individually, then share with their partners whatever they are comfortable sharing from the worksheet.

Wrap-Up

Bring the whole group back together and ask a few students to share what they wrote or drew on their worksheets and discussed with their partners. Discuss: **We sometimes have stronger feelings**

than needed when we are in the middle of a difficult situation. When time has passed, we can look back and say to ourselves, "Maybe I didn't need to get that upset."

Say: **If we take the last few lessons together—doing a body scan, using the stress meter, and noticing our feelings' volume—we can learn how to notice our body signals and adjust our feelings' volume to match what is happening. Often when we do this, we can lower our stress level and handle the situation more calmly.**

Write the following steps on the whiteboard and review them with students:

1. Scan your body.

2. What stress level is your feeling on a scale of 1 to 10?

3. Does the level match the situation? Does it seem too loud?

As a review, ask students what coping skills they could use to lower their feelings' volume. Elicit answers like *belly breathing* and *practicing the Pause.* Let them know that they will be learning more skills to adjust their feelings' volume.

Mindful Checkout

Invite students to find a comfortable position and sit quietly. Choose one of these activities to guide your students through a mindful checkout, referencing "Mindful Pauses to Begin and End Lessons" on page 17 for guidance as needed:

- Practice the Pause
- Be Mindful of Change

Follow-Up

Practice variations of the three steps in the Wrap-Up with your class when you notice students starting to get upset. Ask a sequence of questions like: **What are you feeling? What level is it from 1 to 10? Do you think it matches the situation?** Sometimes, students will be willing and able to adjust their feelings' volume in the moment. Other times, they may need time for emotions to settle and some distance from the incident before they can reflect back on it. That's okay. Do not try to convince them to lower their feelings' level in the moment. Following up in this way gradually gets students into the practice of becoming more aware in the moment (practicing mindfulness).

Considerations

If you have students with sensitivity to sound, allow them to leave the room or put on headphones before you play the loud music at the start of this activity. Give them a heads-up about the scene during the mini play when one student is exaggerating their feeling, and again give them options such as leaving the room, wearing headphones, or simply covering their ears during this scene.

FEELING TOO LOUD

Scenario 1: The Spill

Juan accidentally spills juice on Lydia's backpack.

Scenario 2: Left Out at Recess

Steven and Keiko are good friends. But today, Keiko played with Aliya at recess instead of Steven. Steven is talking to Keiko after recess.

Scenario 3: Forgot My Homework

Milo did not complete the homework that was due today. Milo's teacher, Ms. Ruiz, tells them that they will have to stay inside to finish it instead of going out for recess with the rest of the class.

Name:_____ Date:_____

From *Teaching Kids to Pause, Cope, and Connect: Lessons for Social-Emotional Learning and Mindfulness* by Mark Purcell, Psy.D., and Kellen Glinder, M.D., copyright © 2022. This page may be reproduced for individual, classroom, or small group work only. For other uses, contact Free Spirit Publishing at freespirit.com/permissions.

ADJUST YOUR FEELINGS' VOLUME

Think of a time when you got more upset than you meant to. Describe what happened below, or draw a picture of it.

1. On the stress meter scale of 1 to 10, how upset did you feel at the time? _____

2. Think back to that time now. What level on the stress meter scale of 1 to 10 do you think would be appropriate for the situation? _____

3. Do you think things would have gone differently if your feeling level was at that appropriate stress level? Yes _____ No _____

4. What would you have done differently if your feeling level had been at that lower level?

5. How might other people have acted differently if you'd expressed that level of feeling?

Name:_____ Date:_____

From *Teaching Kids to Pause, Cope, and Connect: Lessons for Social-Emotional Learning and Mindfulness* by Mark Purcell, Psy.D., and Kellen Glinder, M.D., copyright © 2022. This page may be reproduced for individual, classroom, or small group work only. For other uses, contact Free Spirit Publishing at freespirit.com/permissions.

LIFE SKILL V
BE CALM

When kids are able to calm their bodies and minds, they are better prepared to work through strong feelings. Kids who regularly practice relaxation strategies develop muscle memory that can prompt them to calm themselves down during stressful times.

When kids are overwhelmed by feelings, they go into what we call *emotional mind*. When this happens, their rational mind, which normally regulates emotions, goes off-line. We call this being *dysregulated*. In this state, the rational mind cannot communicate with the emotional mind. Trying to reason with a child who is dysregulated is like speaking to them in a different language. It can even feel invalidating and cause more frustration. It's often better to give them the space to calm down or guide them in using self-soothing strategies to regulate their physical and emotional systems.

Introducing This Life Skill to Students

There are various options for introducing the Be Calm life skill based on the needs of your group and your time limitations. The following lessons provide different learning experiences related to being calm. If you are limited on time, you can start with the first lesson. Otherwise, you can introduce the skill with quotations and class discussion or by reading related books.

1. **Quotations and Socratic Questioning:** You may start a brief discussion by reading one of the quotations listed below (or another one chosen by you).

   • "I cannot always control what goes on outside. But I can always control what goes on inside."—Wayne Dyer

   • "Learn to calm down the winds of your mind, and you will enjoy great inner peace." —Remez Sasson

- "Look at a tree, a flower, a plant. Let your awareness rest upon it. How still they are, how deeply rooted in Being. Allow nature to teach you stillness." —Eckhart Tolle

Follow up your chosen quotation with questions such as:

- What does this quotation mean to you?
- How does it relate to the life skill of being calm?
- Why do you think it is important to stay calm or be able to calm down?
- Can you share a time when you calmed down?

2. **Related Literature:** You may wish to connect this life skill to relevant children's literature. You can begin a lesson by reading one of the books listed below, or you can read parts of it between the three lessons related to this life skill.
   - *The Lemonade Hurricane* by Licia Morelli
   - *Good Morning Yoga: A Pose-by-Pose Wake Up Story* by Mariam Gates

Further Resources

- "How to Help Children Calm Down" by Caroline Miller, childmind.org/article/how-to-help-children-calm-down
- "Calming Children: Self Calming Strategies" by Carrie Clark, speechandlanguagekids.com/calming-children-self-calming-strategies

LESSON 13
THE SQUEEZE AND MINDFUL STRETCHING (PAUSE)

Lesson Summary

Students will learn a form of muscle relaxation called the Squeeze, which they can easily do almost anywhere to release tension and calm down. Students will also learn basic yoga and mindful stretching to relax.

Keywords

- the Squeeze
- relaxation
- mindful stretching
- yoga

Students Will

- learn a simple muscle relaxation skill to reduce stress
- learn basic yoga poses and mindful stretches

Materials

- "Mindful Stretching" handout
- a few rubber bands

Mindful Check-In

Guide students through the Pause for a mindful check-in, referencing "Mindful Pauses to Begin and End Lessons" on page 17 for guidance as needed.

Activity

Explain to students that the next activity will teach them how to use their bodies to calm themselves down quickly. Explain: **The Squeeze can help you relax when you feel worried or stressed. It can also help you calm down when you start to feel upset.**

The Squeeze

1. Instruct students to stand up and rest their hands loosely at their sides.

2. Ask them to do a quick body scan to notice how they feel.

3. Invite students to squeeze all their muscles from their fists to their toes. You might also invite them to scrunch up their faces while they do the Squeeze.

4. Ask them to hold the Squeeze while they take a deep belly breath to a count of three.

5. Then say "Release." The students should release their fists and tensed muscles.

6. Repeat the exercise three times, saying, **"Breathe in. Squeeze tighter, tighter, tighter. And release."**

Ask students whether they noticed a difference in how their bodies felt before and after doing the Squeeze.

Mindful Stretching

Explain: **When we practice mindful stretching, we use our bodies to train our minds. To hold each pose, we need to keep our minds focused on our bodies. Mindful stretching makes a connection between body and mind.**

Stretch out rubber bands and say: **Your muscles are like rubber bands. When you gently stretch them out, then gently release the stretch, your whole body relaxes. And you will find that your mind feels calm and relaxed in the same way.**

Direct students to the "Mindful Stretching" handout, which shows illustrations of the four basic mindful stretching poses. Lead students through each of the four poses individually.

STAR POSE

Stand with feet apart and arms spread out and up so your body forms a big X. Your hands, feet, and head become the five points of a star. Hold the pose for five to ten of your own slow breaths, depending on the ability and attention span of the students. Older students may be able to pose longer, but younger students may need demonstrations, individualized instruction, and practice to get into a sustainable star pose.

FIGURE 3: FROG POSE

FROG POSE

With feet flat on the floor, squat down. Press your palms or fingertips into the floor between your knees, like a frog preparing to jump. Hold this pose for five to ten breaths, depending on the comfort of your students (again, older students will be able to hold this longer).

RAINBOW POSE

From frog pose, spring up to standing position with your left arm at your side and your right hand raised high. Next, slowly lean to the left, like your body is an arching rainbow with your right arm extending the curve.

After five to ten breaths in rainbow pose, slowly return to frog pose for another round of breathing. Then spring up again, this time with your right arm at your side and your left arm up and arching to the

FIGURE 2: STAR POSE

FIGURE 4: RAINBOW POSE

right. Lean to the right. Again, hold for five to ten breaths.

RAGDOLL POSE
Lastly, slump forward with straight legs but loose arms and neck drooping to the ground like a ragdoll for five to ten breaths. This completes the core mindful stretching cycle.

FIGURE 5: RAGDOLL POSE

Once students know the poses, lead them through the full cycle: star, frog, rainbow, and ragdoll. If time allows, it can help to repeat the full cycle a couple of times. Usually, going through the cycle three times is enough to get a full effect for most students, but the cycle can be repeated more times if desired.

Wrap-Up

Explain: **You can use the Squeeze when your Stress Meter is high or when you think you should lower your feelings' volume. Mindful stretching can help you relax your muscles and calm your mind. You can also use the Squeeze and mindful stretching to help you relax at night before you go to sleep.**

Mindful Checkout

Invite students to find a comfortable position and sit quietly. Choose one of these activities to guide your students through a mindful checkout, referencing "Mindful Pauses to Begin and End Lessons" on page 17 for guidance as needed:

- Practice the Pause
- Be Mindful of Change

Follow-Up

You can use the Squeeze during stretch breaks throughout the day. This relatively quick activity can help students relax, wake up, or release restless energy. When you have a little more time, use mindful stretching to help students relieve stress or find more focus.

Variation
Full-Body Progressive Relaxation

You can do a longer, full-body version of the Squeeze. If possible, have students lie down on their backs. Just like in the body scan, start at the feet, then slowly move through each part of the body. For each area, guide students as you did with the Squeeze—tightening a particular muscle or area of the body for a count of three, then releasing.

Considerations

You may need to modify this activity for students with physical limitations. One possible modification is "chair yoga," which students can do while seated. Some chair yoga poses are demonstrated by Yoga Ed. at youtube.com/watch?v=Pbhr0TMmg9I.

MINDFUL STRETCHING

Star Pose

Rainbow Pose

Frog Pose

Ragdoll Pose

Name:_____ Date:_____

From *Teaching Kids to Pause, Cope, and Connect: Lessons for Social-Emotional Learning and Mindfulness* by Mark Purcell, Psy.D., and Kellen Glinder, M.D., copyright © 2022. This page may be reproduced for individual, classroom, or small group work only. For other uses, contact Free Spirit Publishing at freespirit.com/permissions.

LESSON 14
SOOTHE WITH THE SENSES (COPE)

Lesson Summary

In this activity, students will experiment with different materials and experiences that engage the senses. Students will learn how these types of sensory self-soothing can be calming and reduce emotional distress.

Keywords

- self-soothe
- five senses

Students Will

- learn how to self-soothe by using the five senses
- understand how self-soothing with the senses can relax the body
- identify the types of materials and experiences that they find soothing

Materials

- "What Feels Good to Me" handout
- five containers
- materials to set up stations that engage each of the five senses, such as:
  1. Sight: postcards of pleasant images
  2. Hearing: bell, rain stick, instruments. *Optional*: If feasible, allow options to listen to music, as many students find this self-soothing. You may

want to provide headphones or a small speaker connected to a device that can play music. Alternatively, you may choose to allow students at that station to play music on their own devices. If you allow this, encourage students to pick music that is relatively calm or music without lyrics.

  3. Taste: fruit, small pieces of chocolate or hard candy
  4. Smell: flower petals, essential oils
  5. Touch: different types of cloth, sand, marbles, clay

- *optional*: a bell or other alarm (clapping or using your voice works too)

Preparation

- Arrange the room so that you have five different stations, and label each station with one of the five senses. You can simply write the names of the senses on pieces of paper, or you can draw images on the paper to identify the sense for each station.
- At each station, place a container with the items for that sense.

Save the objects from this activity for the next lesson, Find Your Calm Space.

Mindful Check-In

Guide students through the Pause for a mindful check-in, referencing "Mindful Pauses to Begin and End Lessons" on page 17 for guidance as needed.

Activity

Explain: **Doing things that connect us with our senses can relax our bodies. As we've learned, a relaxed body can calm our feelings when we are upset.** Ask students to name the five senses: sight, hearing, taste, smell, and touch.

Divide students into five groups. Explain that they are going to rotate through the stations to explore the different materials. Encourage students to try to do this activity in a calm, quiet manner. Remind students to be respectful of each other and of the materials that they are exploring.

Soothe with the Senses Activity

1. Tell students that they will have two to three minutes at each station to explore what is there.

2. Ask them to use their detective skills to notice what they feel through their senses at each station.

3. Assign each group to one of the five stations.

4. Inform students that you will ring a bell (or use any other signal) when it's time to begin and again when it's time to move to the next station. Tell them which direction to move when the bell rings. (You might number each station so students go sequentially, or you may have the stations arranged in a clear circle).

5. Tell students that you would like them to slowly take all the items out of the container when the bell rings.

6. Ring the bell.

7. Guide students with the following prompts:

   - Say: **Look over the objects at the station.**

   - Say: **Pick one item and focus your attention on how it feels to the sense your station is about.**

   - Remind students about the Be a Detective lesson (page 43). Encourage them to notice, observe, and then describe (silently). Remind them to avoid labels or judgments like "This stinks" or "This is gross."

   - Say: **Take time to really notice how the object looks, sounds, tastes, smells, or feels.**

   - Say: **Take turns passing objects around to each other and exploring them.**

8. Ring the bell (or use your chosen signal) and instruct students to move to the next station. They can leave the objects laid out on the table for the next group to explore.

9. Repeat until students have completed all five stations.

10. Ask students to spend a few minutes completing the "What Feels Good to Me" handout.

Wrap-Up

Ask for a few students to share what they explored and experienced. Encourage them to practice their detective skills and describe what they noticed. Ask: **Did different objects or experiences spark**

different emotions in you? Did some help you feel calm? Did others spark feelings of nervousness or discomfort? Elicit a few answers. Encourage students to use their senses to notice things in their surroundings to self-soothe, both at school and at home.

Follow-Up

Suggest that students bring home the lists they created on the "What Feels Good to Me" handout. Encourage them to gather similar objects at home that they can use to self-soothe. They may even create their own box or container of soothing things. Invite students to use these objects to calm themselves when they're feeling upset. Encourage students to keep adding new activities that engage the five senses to their lists, such as petting their pets, cooking, or going to the beach.

Considerations

Before setting up this activity, check with students and families to find out if students have any specific allergies, and ensure you do not include these items. These can include types of food, essential oils, certain fabrics, or items found in nature (such as wool or grass).

Consider students who may have sensory issues, and adjust the stations or provide additional guidance as appropriate. For example, you may need to ask students to play instruments softly if you have students with sensory sensitivities to loud noise.

WHAT FEELS GOOD TO ME

Think of different things that feel good to you and that you might use to calm yourself down. Write down or draw a picture of each thing next to the sense it uses.

Sense	What Feels, Sounds, Tastes, Looks, and Smells Good to Me
Touch	
Sight	
Sounds	
Taste	
Smell	

Name:_____ Date:_____

From *Teaching Kids to Pause, Cope, and Connect: Lessons for Social-Emotional Learning and Mindfulness* by Mark Purcell, Psy.D., and Kellen Glinder, M.D., copyright © 2022. This page may be reproduced for individual, classroom, or small group work only. For other uses, contact Free Spirit Publishing at freespirit.com/permissions.

LESSON 15
FIND YOUR CALM SPACE (CONNECT)

Lesson Summary

In this fun group project, students work together in small groups to design their own "calm space."

Keywords

- calm space
- taking a time-out

Students Will

- learn the importance of setting up their own calm space
- identify environments and activities that can create a calm space

Materials

- containers of sensory objects from the previous activity, Soothe with the Senses
- a range of household objects that can be used for setting up a comfortable space, such as pillows, soft blankets, or pieces of carpet
- classroom objects that can be used for calming activities, such as books, fidgets, instruments, or headphones

Mindful Check-In

Guide students through the Pause for a mindful check-in, referencing "Mindful Pauses to Begin and End Lessons" on page 17 for guidance as needed.

Activity

Explain: **Having your own space away from others, with things to do that calm you, can be very important for dealing with Big Feelings. In this activity, you're going use different kinds of objects from home and school to set up your ideal calm space getaway.**

Ask students to describe places they go or things they do alone that help them relax.

Explain: **When you are getting upset, it often involves other people—classmates, family members, or even teachers. It can help to take a break, like a time-out. Finding a calm space where you can do your own thing can be very helpful.** If you have it, direct students to the glitter jar from the first lesson. Shake it up and explain that a calm space can be where we can allow our strong feelings to settle.

Calm Space Activity

1. Divide students into groups of four or five. Assign each group an area in the classroom where they can set up their calm space.

2. Direct students to the five containers with objects from the Soothe with the Senses lesson. Show students some

98

of the additional objects that you brought for the activity.

3. First, ask the groups to simply inspect the different objects that are available.

4. Then, have each group plan out how they would like to create their calm space.

5. Encourage students to be creative and remind them to include ways to engage all their senses.

6. Tell groups that they will have ten minutes to design and set up their calm spaces, then invite them to begin.

7. Walk around the room, supporting groups and helping them design their spaces. You may also need to help groups negotiate and compromise when they disagree about what objects they want to place in their space, or which group gets which objects.

8. Give a two-minute warning. Then after ten minutes, ring a bell.

9. Encourage each group to think up a name for their special calm space. Give them a few moments to discuss within their groups.

10. Ask each group to give a tour of their calm space to the rest of the class.

11. Congratulate them all on their teamwork and creativity.

Wrap-Up

Summarize how important it is that we can find our own calm places to go to when we are having a tough time or when we just need our own space. Say: **Some of you may have your own room to go to. Some of you may not because you share a room. The size of our calm space**

doesn't matter as much as how we use it. Sometimes, our calm space can simply be a corner of a room where we draw, read, or listen to calming music.

Discuss some of the important aspects of our calm spaces. Say: **We go there with the intention of calming down and to have our own space, not to storm there with anger or go on our cell phones and angrily text someone.** Ask students what kinds of activities would disrupt their calmness.

Say: **Remember to be respectful when you ask others to give you your space. At home, you can ask your parents to let you go to your calm space when you are feeling upset.**

Remind students that their calm space cannot be used to completely avoid consequences after a conflict or bad situation. Sometimes, they will have to come back to some difficult conversations after they calm down.

Mindful Checkout

Invite students to find a comfortable position and sit quietly. Choose one of these activities to guide your students through a mindful checkout, referencing "Mindful Pauses to Begin and End Lessons" on page 17 for guidance as needed:

- Practice the Pause
- Be Mindful of Change

Follow-Up

If space is available, you may decide to keep a designated calm space in your classroom with its own creative name. Many teachers have found this to be very

helpful for students to use when they are upset or simply need a break because they find the classroom overstimulating. You may wish to include items like pillows, carpets, blankets, and stuffed animals, as well as sleep masks to cover the eyes or sound-muffling headphones. Try to avoid having electronic gadgets or screens in the calm space, except for headphones that may play relaxing music, nature sounds, or audio books. Ideally, students should be able to access this space when they need to de-escalate while not abusing the privilege, so use your own judgment in deciding how often you'll allow the students to access this space and how long they can remain there each time.

If creating a classroom calm space isn't feasible, encourage students to have access to items for activities they like to do alone that calm them down and that you allow them to use during lessons. These may include books, drawing materials, or fidgets.

Variation
Classroom Calm Space

Instead of having groups of students create separate calm spaces, you can use this activity to create one permanent calm space for use in your classroom (see the "Follow-Up" instructions for this lesson for guidance on keeping a permanent calm space). Use this activity to design, create, and decorate your classroom calm space together, soliciting ideas from students and making decisions as a team about what will work best in your classroom and cause minimal disruption. You might keep some of the objects from the Soothe with the Senses lesson in the space. You can continue to add to the classroom calm space over time as students identify other items and activities that they find calming.

Considerations

Make any needed adjustments for food allergies or sensory sensitivities (see considerations in previous activity, Soothe with the Senses).

LIFE SKILL VI
BE CREATIVE

Being creative is a natural tendency that children are born with and that fosters healthy development. From a young age, children use creativity and curiosity to explore their surroundings. Unfortunately, at some stages in development, many students experience judgment and become self-critical. As a result, they may stifle their creativity with phrases like "I can't draw," "I can't dance," and so on. It's important to emphasize the power of creativity itself rather than focusing on the final product.

Creativity is an important aspect of many areas that are essential to healthy development. Creative expression allows people to communicate and process their emotions. The development of a growth mindset relies upon creativity and critical thinking. Creativity has also been proven to be a necessary ingredient in problem-solving. In addition to these benefits, creativity can be a wonderful tool for mindfulness and relaxation.

Introducing This Life Skill to Students

There are various options for introducing the Be Creative life skill based on the needs of your group and your time limitations. The following lessons provide learning experiences related to Being Creative. If you are limited on time, you can start with the first lesson. Otherwise, you can introduce the skill with quotations and class discussion or by reading related books.

1. **Quotations and Socratic Questioning:** You may start a brief discussion by reading one of the quotations listed below (or another one chosen by you).

   - "You can't use up creativity. The more you use, the more you have." —Maya Angelou

   - "Creativity is intelligence having fun." —Adapted from George Scialabba

   - "Creativity is a wild mind and a disciplined eye." —Dorothy Parker

Follow up your chosen quotation with questions such as:

- What does this quotation mean to you?
- How does it relate to the life skill of being creative?
- Why do you think it is important to use your creativity?
- Can you share a time when you were creative?

2. **Related Literature:** You may wish to connect this life skill to relevant children's literature. You can begin a lesson by reading one of the books listed below, or you can read parts of it between the three lessons related to this life skill.

- *The Dot* by Peter H. Reynolds
- *The Day the Crayons Quit* by Drew Daywalt
- *What Do You Do with an Idea?* by Kobi Yomada

Further Resources

- Sylvia Duckworth's "12 Benefits of Creativity" infographic, listed in "My Top 10 Sketchnotes in 2016," sylviaduckworth.com/2016/12/28/top-10-sketchnotes-2016
- "The Importance of Fostering Creativity in the Classroom" by Carly Daff, medium.com/canva/the-importance-of-fostering-creativity-in-the-classroom-34c94b99281d
- "The Positive Benefits of Creativity" by Nicola Vanlint, lifelabs.psychologies.co.uk/posts/4292-the-positive-benefits-of-creativity

LESSON 16
DRAWING TO MUSIC (PAUSE)

Lesson Summary

Students will draw while they listen to very different types of music. This mindfulness activity will show how we can have different "feeling tones" related to what we experience.

Keywords

- mindfulness of feelings
- feeling tones

Students Will

- draw to different types of music
- learn about different feeling tones they can have
- understand that feelings can be affected by what they experience around them

Materials

- crayons, markers, and/or colored pencils and paper (two or three pieces per student, depending on number of music selections)
- two or three very different music selections (see suggestions under "Preparation")
- device for playing music recordings

Preparation

To prepare for this mindfulness activity, select two or three songs that are very different from each other. For longer songs,

limit yourself to two-to-three-minute segments. Try to pick songs that do not have lyrics, as these can distract or lead to students drawing the given story instead of their felt experience.

Possible music selections:

- Classical: Beethoven's Fifth Symphony, Tchaikovsky's "1812 Overture" or "Waltz of the Flowers"
- Jazz: "Alabama" by John Coltrane, "The Entertainer" by Scott Joplin, "'Round Midnight" by Thelonious Monk
- Electronic: "Anasthasia" by Deep Forest, "Buenos Aires" by Nick Warren, "Sonic Kipper" by Atmos
- Indigenous: "Cumbias" by Inca Son, "Eagle Song" by Red Shadow Singers, "Mother Earth" by Wuauquikuna

Mindful Check-In

Guide students through the Pause for a mindful check-in, referencing "Mindful Pauses to Begin and End Lessons" on page 17 for guidance as needed.

Activity

Arrange seating so that students have space to draw. This can be at their desks or tables with their own art materials or at a table in groups of four or five with materials to share.

Drawing to Music Activity

1. Tell students that you are going to play some different types of music. Explain: **Draw along with the music on one of your pieces of paper. You can draw whatever you like as the music plays. Don't feel like you need to draw a certain picture. You have the freedom to draw squiggles and shapes.**

2. Play the first selection for about two minutes.

3. Give students a warning when about thirty seconds remain.

4. When the selection ends, have students use a new piece of paper. Tell students that you are going to change to a different song and instruct them to draw along to the new music.

5. Play the second selection. After about two minutes, give students a thirty-second warning.

6. When the selection ends, ask students to stop drawing.

7. *Optional*: If time allows, you can repeat this process with a third song.

Ask for a volunteer to share the drawings they made to each of the types of music. The drawings will likely be very different from each other in some ways.

Ask: **Why do you think these drawings are so different?** Discuss how music can make us feel many things.

Try to get a few more examples of drawings from students, noticing the different styles and images they may show. As they share their drawings, ask students to try to describe how each selection of music made them feel. Write some of these descriptions on the whiteboard.

Explain: **This mindfulness activity shows us how we can have different "feeling tones." Think of feeling tones as the experience a feeling creates for us. For example, one of these songs might have slow, deep sounds. It might create a feeling of sadness or of missing someone. These are unpleasant feeling tones. Another song may be fast and energetic and create an excited or happy feeling. This is a pleasant feeling tone. There are also neutral feeling tones. An important part of mindfulness is noticing our feeling tones.**

Wrap-Up

Ask students to take a few belly breaths. Then instruct them to pay attention to what feeling tones they are having right now. Have students close their eyes or direct a soft gaze downward.

Say: **See if you can notice your own special feeling tones. If you pay attention, you might notice that your feelings are always changing, just like the music we were listening to. You might also see colors or images like the drawings you made to the music.** Pause for thirty seconds to one minute.

Explain: **Sometimes our emotions can be so powerful they feel like a huge tidal wave, like they can sweep us away. And we might feel like we are fighting to control them or push them away. But if we learn to simply observe our feeling tones, we realize that they are always changing, just like the weather. And if we let go of trying to control them, we can watch them change. The stormy anger we feel one moment can turn into sunny happiness later.**

Mindful Checkout

Invite students to find a comfortable position and sit quietly. Choose one of these activities to guide your students through a mindful checkout, referencing "Mindful Pauses to Begin and End Lessons" on page 17 for guidance as needed:

- Practice the Pause
- Be Mindful of Change

Follow-Up

You can repeat this mindfulness activity throughout the week using different types of music.

LESSON 17
DRAW SOLUTIONS (COPE)

Lesson Summary

In this lesson, students will learn how to solve problems by using their imaginations.

Keywords

- problems
- solutions
- drawing

Students Will

- learn how to apply their imagination to problems in their lives
- learn a new way to approach problems and develop solutions

Materials

- crayons, markers, and/or colored pencils
- three pieces of paper per student
- *for Looking at Problems Differently activity variation*: "Thinking Outside the Box" handout

Preparation

- Divide the whiteboard into three different panels to draw on, and number them 1, 2, and 3.

Mindful Check-In

Guide students through the Pause for a mindful check-in, referencing "Mindful Pauses to Begin and End Lessons" on page 17 for guidance as needed.

Activity

Explain: **Did you know that creativity is part of problem-solving? Sometimes we can't solve a problem because we can only see one way to solve it.** Ask students to share times they solved a problem in a new and different way.

Explain: **This fun coping skill will teach you how to use your imagination to help you solve problems and challenges.**

Drawing Solutions Activity

1. Ask students to prepare the three pieces of paper you've distributed. Have them number the sheets 1, 2, and 3 at the top of the page.

2. Invite students to think of a problem they're dealing with. It can be just about any kind of problem in their lives.

3. On the whiteboard, draw an example of a problem in the panel labeled "1." For example, you could draw a picture of getting to school late (yourself or a fictional student). This might be a stick figure running in the door with a clock above, and then the

phrase "Being Late" written beneath the picture.

4. Instruct students to draw a picture of their own problems on the paper numbered "1." Say: **You can draw the problem in any way that you want and include whoever you like in the picture.** Remind students not to worry about how good or bad their drawing is. This is more about using their imaginations.

5. Give students three minutes to draw. You can walk around the room to help students who may be having difficulties.

6. When they finish, ask them to write "My Problem" at the top.

7. Say: **Now, imagine what it would look like if your problem were solved.**

8. Draw an example of the problem solved on the whiteboard in the panel labeled "3." Using the above example, this could be you or the fictional student arriving to school on time.

9. Invite students to draw their pictures of their problems solved on the paper numbered "3." Say: **Use your imagination to show what it would look and feel like if your problem were solved.**

10. Give students three minutes to complete this drawing. Walk around the room to provide guidance and encouragement.

11. When they finish, ask them to write "Problem Solved" at the top of the page.

12. Say: **Now that you know what it looks like when your problem is solved, ask yourself, "How can I get there?" You're going to use your**

imagination to figure out a way you to get from "My Problem" to "Problem Solved."

13. On the board, draw an example of how you (or the fictional student) could get from picture 1 ("My Problem") to picture 3 ("Problem Solved"). An example might be drawing someone getting out of bed with an alarm clock nearby. Underneath you might write something like "Get up earlier." Or you could draw a person putting things into a backpack and write "Get stuff ready the night before" underneath.

14. Ask students to take out the paper numbered "2." Invite them to come up with a creative way to get from picture 1 ("My Problem") to picture 3 ("Problem Solved") and draw it out. For this part, you may want to divide students into pairs so they can ask a partner for suggestions if they get stuck.

15. Say: **Remember, this is an opportunity to be creative. Your drawing can be something that can really happen. Or it could be something you make up using your imagination.** *Note: It is important that students are allowed to make up solutions that range from realistic to fantastic. When possible, it is great if students come up with a realistic solution they can apply to their problem. However, some problems may be very hard to solve realistically (for example, loss of a loved one). So give students the choice to use their imagination as well.*

16. If you have students work in pairs, encourage them to first to try and come up with a solution by themselves. Then after a minute or two,

see if their partner can provide some additional suggestions.

17. Give students five minutes to complete this drawing activity. Circle the room to provide them with guidance and encouragement.

Wrap-Up

Ask students if any of them were surprised by the solutions they came up with. Ask for a few examples, and have volunteers share their three drawings. Say: **Sometimes we think there is only one way to solve a problem, and we keep trying that way over and over. It often takes looking at a situation or problem in a new way to find the best solution. Next time you face a problem, try to ask yourself, "Is there a different way this problem can be solved?"**

Follow-Up

During the next week, when students face difficulties, encourage them to consider different ways to solve the problem. You can also follow up this activity by having students complete the "Thinking Outside the Box" handout (see variation).

Variation
Looking at Problems Differently

You can add this variation to the beginning or the end of the lesson. If time is limited, you can replace the art-based activity with this version. Direct students to the "Thinking Outside the Box" handout. Copy the diagram onto the whiteboard. Ask students to try to figure out how to solve the puzzle. Give them about three minutes. If no one solves the puzzle, show them the solution on the board. (The solution to the puzzle is printed on the "Thinking Outside the Box Solution" teacher resource.) Lead a discussion about how creativity is related to solving problems. It sometimes takes looking at a problem in a new way to find the solution. Ask students for examples of times they solved a problem in a new way.

Considerations

If a student chooses to draw a problem in their lives that is very serious, check in with a school counselor or psychologist to ensure the student is properly supported.

THINKING OUTSIDE THE BOX

Try to link all nine dots using four straight lines or fewer without lifting the pen and without tracing back over any of your lines.

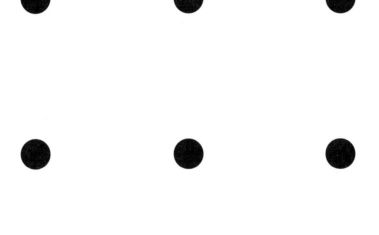

Name:_____ Date:_____

From *Teaching Kids to Pause, Cope, and Connect: Lessons for Social-Emotional Learning and Mindfulness* by Mark Purcell, Psy.D., and Kellen Glinder, M.D., copyright © 2022. This page may be reproduced for individual, classroom, or small group work only. For other uses, contact Free Spirit Publishing at freespirit.com/permissions.

THINKING OUTSIDE THE BOX SOLUTION

All solutions require the solver to draw a line that extends outside of the "box" formed by the grid.

Solution: The figure shows one solution.

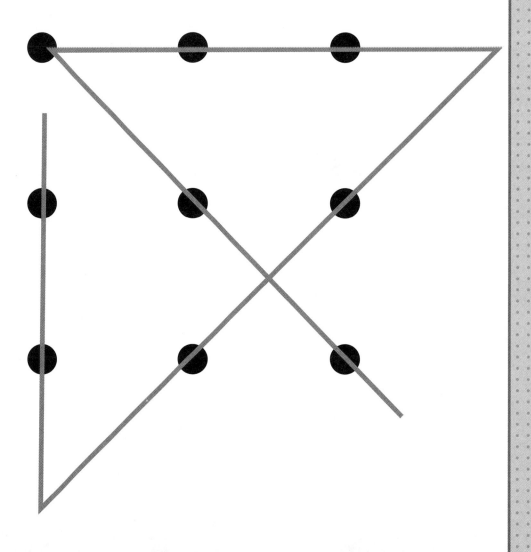

From *Teaching Kids to Pause, Cope, and Connect: Lessons for Social-Emotional Learning and Mindfulness* by Mark Purcell, Psy.D., and Kellen Glinder, M.D., copyright © 2022. This page may be reproduced for individual, classroom, or small group work only. For other uses, contact Free Spirit Publishing at freespirit.com/permissions.

LESSON 18
FEELINGS CHARADES (CONNECT)

Lesson Summary

In this lesson, students will play Feelings Charades to understand how feelings are expressed.

Keywords

- feelings
- feeling zones

Students Will

- understand the ways that feelings are expressed and communicated
- learn the four different feeling zones
- learn how to care for difficult feelings and change feeling zones

Materials

- "How Are You Feeling?" handout

Preparation

- Take four pieces of different-colored paper. In large print, write one of the four feeling zones on each piece of paper: "Angry," "Sad," "Scared," and "Happy/Peaceful."
- Place the four labels in four different area of the classroom.
- Cut out each of the feeling characters on the "How Are You Feeling?" handout, then place them into a container that can be used for Feelings Charades.

Mindful Check-In

Guide students through the Pause for a mindful check-in, referencing "Mindful Pauses to Begin and End Lessons" on page 17 for guidance as needed.

Activity

Explain: **We express how we feel with our words, faces, and bodies. As social beings, we also learn to read what others are feeling based on their facial expressions and actions.**

Feelings Charades Activity (Part 1)

Seat students so everyone is facing the front of the room, leaving a space in front for students to take turns performing.

Explain the rules for playing Feelings Charades:

1. You will call on a volunteer who will come to the "stage" and draw a feeling from the container. (You can whisper the feeling to the actor if they have trouble reading it.)
2. Ask the volunteer to act out the feeling. The audience will try to guess what it is.
3. When they guess it, the students decide which of the four feeling zones that feeling belongs to.
4. The actor then goes to stand in that feeling zone.

Play this part of Feelings Charades until each student who wants to act out a feeling has had a chance, or until the students understand and are ready to move on.

Feelings Charades Activity (Part 2)

Explain: **When we take care of our feelings, we can move from one feeling zone to another.**

1. Ask one of the students to share the feeling they acted out in Feelings Charades. Ask the actor what they could do to move to the Happy/Peaceful Zone. Let other students make suggestions if needed. For example, a student may be acting as the "Tired" feeling in the Sad Zone. She may suggest that that napping would help her care for the tired feeling. After answering what she can do to care for the feeling, the actor moves over to the Happy/Peaceful Zone of the room.

2. Continue to play this extension of Feelings Charades for about five minutes. Acknowledge how the Happy/Peaceful group is getting larger.

Wrap-Up

Say: **Remember, no one ever gets sent to the principal's office for what they *feel*. But they may be sent there for what they *do*. As we discussed before, sometimes the volume of our feelings is too strong. If we identify feelings when they're happening and try to do something to move ourselves into the Happy/Peaceful Zone, then we can help stop ourselves from doing something that could hurt ourselves or others.**

Sometimes, just sharing what we are feeling with someone else, like when we have a good cry with a friend or tell an adult about our fears, can shift us from being upset to the Happy/Peaceful Zone.

There is a reason for every feeling. It's important to try to understand each feeling we have and what it is trying to teach us. Then we can take action in the best way.

Mindful Checkout

Invite students to find a comfortable position and sit quietly. Choose one of these activities to guide your students through a mindful checkout, referencing "Mindful Pauses to Begin and End Lessons" on page 17 for guidance as needed:

*   Practice the Pause
*   Be Mindful of Change

Follow-Up

If you wish, hang up a poster-size version of the "How Are You Feeling?" handout. Many variations of it are available at teacher supply stores and online, such as at mymoodsmychoices.com/products/mood-posters. Throughout the week, you can ask students to simply identify how they are feeling by pointing to an image on the poster. If needed, read the name of the feeling to students. This repetition can help students develop a broader emotional vocabulary.

HOW ARE YOU FEELING?

 happy

 disappointed

 elated

 angry

 hopeful

 exhausted

 mischievous

 meh

 dismayed

 scared

 upset

 silly

 overwhelmed

 anxious

 content

 relieved

 delighted

 excited

 surprised

 ill

 guilty

 sad

 loved

 bored

 sleepy

Name:_____   Date:_____

From *Teaching Kids to Pause, Cope, and Connect: Lessons for Social-Emotional Learning and Mindfulness* by Mark Purcell, Psy.D., and Kellen Glinder, M.D., copyright © 2022. This page may be reproduced for individual, classroom, or small group work only. For other uses, contact Free Spirit Publishing at freespirit.com/permissions.

LIFE SKILL VII
BE PROUD

Pride and self-confidence promote emotional well-being, resilience, and a growth mindset. When kids feel good about themselves, they have the confidence to try new things and overcome mistakes and momentary failures. When they can take pride in their accomplishments, they are more likely to put forth their best effort. And when kids feel secure about who they are, they tend to be more accepting of others. High self-esteem promotes more flexibility, creativity, curiosity, and critical thinking. Kids who approach situations with an attitude of confidence and competence are more willing to take on new challenges and encourage others to do the same (Burnette et al. 2019).

Introducing This Life Skill to Students

There are various options for introducing the Be Proud life skill to students based on the needs of your group and your time limitations. The following lessons provide different learning experiences related to being proud. If you are limited on time, you can start with the first lesson. Otherwise, you can introduce the skill with quotations and class discussion or by reading related books.

1. **Quotations and Socratic Questioning:** You may start a brief discussion by reading one of the quotations listed below (or another one chosen by you).

   - "With confidence you have won even before you have started." —Marcus Garvey

   - "You gain strength, courage, and confidence by every experience in which you really stop to look fear in the face." —Eleanor Roosevelt

   - "The most beautiful thing you can wear is confidence." —Blake Lively

Follow up your chosen quotation with questions such as:

- What does this quotation mean to you?
- How does it relate to the life skill of being proud?
- Why do you think it is important to have pride in yourself?
- Can you share a time when you were proud of yourself?

2. **Related Literature:** You may wish to connect this life skill to relevant children's literature. You can begin a lesson by reading the book listed below, or you can read parts of it between the three lessons related to this life skill.

   - *I Am Enough* by Grace Byers

Further Resources

- "Your Child's Self-Esteem" by KidsHealth, kidshealth.org/en/parents/self-esteem.html
- "4 Small Ways to Build Confidence in Kids" by Liz Greene, childmind.org/article/4-small-ways-to-build-confidence-in-kids

LESSON 19
SUPERHERO POSE (PAUSE)

Lesson Summary

Students learn how our bodies can reflect how we feel about ourselves. They learn to take superhero poses to energize and build self-confidence.

Keywords

- low-power body positions
- high-power body positions
- superhero poses

Students Will

- understand how body posture affects mood and what it communicates to others
- pose like various superheroes
- observe how the poses make them feel and what they tell others

Materials

- "Superhero Poses" handout

Mindful Check-In

Guide students through the Pause for a mindful check-in, referencing "Mindful Pauses to Begin and End Lessons" on page 17 for guidance as needed.

Activity

Start by talking about how our bodies feel and look when we feel sad, discouraged, and nervous—the poses we make when we think, "I can't do this," or, "I'm no good." Describe these as low-power poses. They're "low-power" because it's as if our energy drains out of us when we sit or stand this way.

You can demonstrate a low-power pose where you take up as little space as possible. You might slouch and pull your shoulders in with your head down. Share a couple of self-statements out loud that could go along with this pose, such as, "I don't have anything important to say," "I'll never be good at this," or "I'll never learn how to do this right."

Then ask the students to take similar poses. Ask: **How does it feel when you sit/stand like this?** Invite students to look around the room at their classmates in similar low-power poses. Ask them to consider what those poses communicate. Ask a few students to share how this low-power posture makes them feel.

Refer students to the "Superhero Poses" handout. Say: **There are also powerful poses that can make you feel strong and confident.**

Superhero Pose Activity

1. Ask students to stand up tall and take a superhero pose that holds a lot of power and energy, maybe a classic Superman or Wonder Woman pose.

2. Demonstrate by placing your fists on your hips, spreading your legs, lifting your chest, and gazing to the heavens, or by lifting both your arms up in a victorious pose.

3. Have students strike the pose of a superhero of their choosing. Ask them to notice how they feel in their chosen superhero stance. Direct students to think about what their posture says about their character.

4. Invite students to look around the room at the superhero poses of their classmates and consider what messages those poses communicate.

5. Have students change poses at least three times, including at least one low-power pose and two superhero poses. Then ask students to observe how they feel and what messages each pose sends.

6. Have students pick the superhero pose that fits best with their own character.

7. Ask them to take the pose, pretend they are the superhero, and say each of the following phrases to themselves, either aloud or with their inner voice:
   - "I can do this!"
   - "I've got this."
   - "I am amazing!"
   - "I'm awesome!"

8. Encourage students to try holding this high-power pose for one to two minutes. This may seem like a long time for students to hold the pose.

But this length of time helps them really feel the shift of physical energy.

9. To keep kids in their poses, you can make it a competition to see who can pose the longest. Or you can count down from 60 or 120 seconds while students pretend to charge up their superpower. Ask students to take deep belly breaths and imagine that their superpower is charging up as they pose. When the countdown reaches zero, they can pretend to fly off to complete their superhero mission.

Wrap-Up

Ask students to pay attention to how they feel now. Ask and discuss: **Did you feel different after posing like a superhero? Did the words of encouragement you told yourself change how you felt? What do you think your poses told others?** Ask students to describe what they felt and thought in response to other classmates' superhero poses.

Follow-Up

You can start the school day by having the students stand in a superhero pose or have students do this at points in the day when their energy levels seem low.

Variation
Superhero Show-and-Tell

If time permits, you can have students take turns introducing their favorite superheroes and striking that hero's favorite poses. Students can describe what they like most about that superhero. This can be an imaginative way for students to get to know each other better, as the

characteristics and superpowers kids identify with often relate to their own personalities or hopes for themselves.

Considerations

Students with physical limitations may have difficulty holding some of the superpower poses. Consider ways that they may be able to hold a pose while seated, or demonstrate how simple movements and expressions, such as raising the chin or making intense eye contact, can convey superpowers.

SUPERHERO POSES

Low-Power Poses

Positions like these convey nervousness and discomfort.

High-Power Poses

Positions like these convey confidence and strength.

Name:_____ Date:_____

Adapted from the work of social psychologist Amy Cuddy as described in "Power to the People" by Jennifer Altmann, *Princeton Alumni Weekly*, April 2, 2014. Reprinted with permission.

From *Teaching Kids to Pause, Cope, and Connect: Lessons for Social-Emotional Learning and Mindfulness* by Mark Purcell, Psy.D., and Kellen Glinder, M.D., copyright © 2022. This page may be reproduced for individual, classroom, or small group work only. For other uses, contact Free Spirit Publishing at freespirit.com/permissions.

LESSON 20
SUPERPOWERS AND STRENGTHS (COPE)

Lesson Summary
Students will identify their personal strengths and draw pictures of themselves as superheroes. They will also practice telling themselves positive messages (affirmations).

Keywords
- strengths
- superpowers
- positive messages
- affirmations

Students Will
- identify their own personal strengths and imagine themselves as unique superheroes
- learn the power of positive messages and affirmations

Materials
- "My Superpowers and Strengths" handout

Mindful Check-In
Guide students through the Pause for a mindful check-in, referencing "Mindful Pauses to Begin and End Lessons" on page 17 for guidance as needed.

Activity
Remind students of the previous lesson, Superhero Pose. Say: **Just like superheroes, every one of us has our own superpowers—our own special skills and abilities. We call these our strengths.**

Ask: **Can someone tell me something you feel you're good at?** Elicit a few answers from students (these can be activities like soccer or math, or these can be personality characteristics like being funny or smart). Say: **Each one of us has different strengths or superpowers. Today we are going to learn about these and share them with each other.**

My Superpowers and Strengths Activity
1. Divide students into groups of four to five.
2. Direct them to the "My Superpowers and Strengths" handout.
3. Explain: **On this worksheet, you can use the space to write down your superpowers and strengths, or you can draw yourself as a superhero. You can choose to do whichever you are most comfortable with, or you can do both! But if you choose to only do the drawing, be sure to show your superhero using some of your superpowers.**

4. Give students five to ten minutes to complete the worksheet.

5. When students have finished, encourage them to try to come up with names for their superheroes.

6. In their small groups, have students share their superheroes with one another, one at a time.

7. Have the groups identify and briefly discuss at least one strength/superpower about the person presenting before they move on to the next person. This can be an example that relates to one of the strengths they named, or it can be a different strength they appreciate about the person.

Wrap-Up

Explain: **It is important that you each learn how to believe in yourselves. One way to do this is to focus on your strengths and superpowers. The word for believing in yourself is *confidence*. Being confident is not the same as bragging or bullying. It is about believing in your own specialness—being your own superhero.**

Mindful Checkout

Invite students to find a comfortable position and sit quietly. Choose one of these activities to guide your students through a mindful checkout, referencing "Mindful Pauses to Begin and End Lessons" on page 17 for guidance as needed:

- Practice the Pause
- Be Mindful of Change

Follow-Up

You may choose to find a place in the classroom where you can post everyone's personal superheroes and their superpowers. Students can also continue to add superpowers/strengths to their superheroes.

Variation
Strengths and Affirmations

This activity is excellent preparation for practicing affirmations. Follow these steps to guide students in a three-to-five-minute mindfulness practice of affirmations:

1. Ask students to sit quietly and practice the Pause to ground themselves.

2. Instruct them to close their eyes or look downward with a soft gaze.

3. Tell them you are going to say statements meant to give them calm confidence.

4. Encourage them to try to "feel" the words in their bodies and to imagine what that looks like in their minds.

5. Say the following affirmations (or your own variations), pausing for twenty or thirty seconds between them for students to fully absorb them:

    a. "I can do this."

    b. "I am a good person."

    c. "My ideas are important."

    d. "My feelings matter."

MY SUPERPOWERS AND STRENGTHS

In the space below, write down some of your own personal superpowers or strengths. These can be things that you are good at, like sports, cooking, or dancing. Or these can be ways that you act, like that you are kind, curious, or funny.

Draw yourself as your own special superhero. Be sure to show yourself using some of your superpowers and strengths.

Name of Your Superhero:_____

Name:_____ Date:_____

From *Teaching Kids to Pause, Cope, and Connect: Lessons for Social-Emotional Learning and Mindfulness* by Mark Purcell, Psy.D., and Kellen Glinder, M.D., copyright © 2022. This page may be reproduced for individual, classroom, or small group work only. For other uses, contact Free Spirit Publishing at freespirit.com/permissions.

LESSON 21
'I' STATEMENTS (CONNECT)

Lesson Summary

Students will learn why "I" statements are better than "you" statements and practice using them to communicate feelings.

Keywords

- "I" statements
- "you" statements
- communication

Students Will

- learn how "you" statements can lead to blame and arguments
- learn to use "I" statements to express what they feel and need

Materials

- "'I' Statements" handout

Mindful Check-In

Guide students through the Pause for a mindful check-in, referencing "Mindful Pauses to Begin and End Lessons" on page 17 for guidance as needed.

Activity

Begin this session with a brief description of "you" statements and "I" statements. Both types describe and discuss conflicts. "You" statements usually begin with "you," then go on to tell a person what

they did or didn't do to cause or worsen a conflict. "I" statements begin with "I" and tell the other person what the speaker thinks or feels and why.

On the board, write the following: "I feel (label an emotion) when (describe an event) because (explain why that event triggers that emotion in you)." *Note: For younger students who may not understand the advanced explanation after "Because," you may choose to simply write a blank line there instead.*

Examples will help get this started. Feel free to customize this based on recent classroom events. Some typical examples might be: "I feel <u>anxious</u> when <u>two people answer at the same time</u> because <u>I can only listen to one person at a time</u>," or "I feel <u>sad</u> when <u>I get wet at recess,</u> because <u>I might get cold later in class</u>."

Give the below examples of "you" statements and ask students to try to turn them into "I" statements.

1. "You" statement: "*You* cut in front of me in line!"

2. "I" statement suggestion: "*I* felt *upset* when *you got into line in front of me* because *I was waiting my turn*."

3. "You" statement: "*You* never give me a turn when we play wall ball!"

4. "I" statement suggestion: "*I* feel *sad and left out* when *you don't let me play* because *I want to play with everyone*."

Turning "You" Statements into "I" Statements Activity

1. Divide the students into pairs. This activity can also be done in groups of three if necessary.

2. Instruct them to take out the "'I' Statements" Handout.

3. Have students work with their partners to turn the "you" statements on the worksheet into "I" statements.

4. Ask each student to make up two "you" statements and write them down on the next part of the worksheet.

5. Invite them to trade papers with their partners.

6. Have students role-play one of the "you" statements to their partner. Encourage students to be emotional and direct when giving their "you" statements.

7. Ask the students in each pair to pause and observe how they feel.

8. After they have role-played, ask them to work together to turn the "you" statement into an "I" statement.

9. Have them role-play the "I" statement.

10. Ask the pairs to pause and notice how they feel.

11. Repeat this until everyone gets a chance to role-play a "you" statement and turn it into an "I" statement.

Lead a discussion about the difference between the two statements. Ask: **How did it feel to have someone say a "you" statement at you? Did it feel different when they said an "I" statement instead?** Ask students if they found it hard to turn "you" statements into "I"

statements. Let them know that learning to make "I" statements takes practice.

Explain: **"I" statements can be helpful in more situations than just when we are upset with someone else. We can also use them to express what we need or how we feel in tough situations.** Direct students to the "I" statement diagram on the board again, and ask for examples of times when "I" statements may be helpful. You may choose to provide a few examples to students to guide them through the process, such as:

- "I feel mad when my mom makes me stop gaming because it's the only time I get to play online with my friends."

- "I felt sad when my best friend moved away because I knew I would miss her."

Wrap-Up

Explain: **Often, we act out how we feel instead of saying it, or we hope others will read our minds and guess how we feel. Sometimes, we blame others for conflicts or for our feelings. "I" statements are important because they let other people know how we feel and why we feel that way. But it takes courage to tell someone how you feel. Practicing "I" statements can help you build up the courage to share your feelings with others. We'll also start learning about having courage in our next lessons.**

Follow-Up

Encourage students to keep practicing "I" statements at school and at home. During conflicts between students, try to get them to express themselves using "I" statements. You may want to post the "I" statement diagram someplace visible in the classroom.

"I" STATEMENTS

Try to change the following "you" statements into "I" statements. Remember to follow the steps for creating "I" statements:

I feel (emotion) when (event) because (explain why that event triggers that emotion in you).

You left me out of the game you were playing with everyone else.

I...

You never give me a chance to play the new video game.

I...

You keep getting better grades on tests than me.

I...

Create your own "I" statements for some other events that have happened to you or that you imagine.

Name:_____ Date:_____

From *Teaching Kids to Pause, Cope, and Connect: Lessons for Social-Emotional Learning and Mindfulness* by Mark Purcell, Psy.D., and Kellen Glinder, M.D., copyright © 2022. This page may be reproduced for individual, classroom, or small group work only. For other uses, contact Free Spirit Publishing at freespirit.com/permissions.

LIFE SKILL VIII
HAVE COURAGE

Courage may come up many times a day for elementary school children. It is important to remember that some kids may need courage to do things that other students perform easily. For example, it may take courage for one child to answer a question in class; another child may need courage to stand up to someone who is acting unkind.

Courage helps children persevere against obstacles and challenges, and in the process, they improve their self-esteem. When children feel capable and confident to make courageous choices, they feel like they have more agency and control. They learn to have some direction in their own lives, rather than letting life happen to them.

Introducing This Life Skill to Students

There are various options for introducing the Have Courage life skill to students based on the needs of your group and your time limitations. The following lessons provide different learning experiences related to having courage. If you are limited on time, you can start with the first lesson. Otherwise, you can introduce the skill with quotations and class discussion or by reading related books.

1. **Quotations and Socratic Questioning:** You may start a brief discussion by reading one of the quotations listed below (or another one chosen by you).

   - "I learned that courage was not the absence of fear, but the triumph over it. . . . The brave man is not he who does not feel afraid, but he who conquers that fear." —Nelson Mandela

   - "He who is brave is free." —Seneca

   - "Heroes are people who face down their fears. It is that simple." —David Gemmell

Follow up your chosen quotation with questions such as:

- What does this quotation mean to you?
- What does it mean to Have Courage or be brave?
- How does this quotation relate to the life skill of having courage?
- Why do you think it is important to Have Courage?
- Can you share a time when you were brave?

2. **Related Literature:** You may wish to connect this life skill to relevant children's literature. You can begin a lesson by reading one of the books listed below, or you can read parts of it between the three lessons related to this life skill.

- *Ruby Finds a Worry* by Tom Percival
- *When You Are Brave* by Pat Zietlow Miller

Further Resources

- Hey Sigmund (website) by Karen Young, heysigmund.com

LESSON 22
SPIDEY SENSE: MINDFULNESS OF SOUND (PAUSE)

Lesson Summary
In this lesson, students learn to apply mindful awareness to sounds.

Keywords
- Spidey Sense
- mindfulness of sound

Students Will
- learn to focus attention on sounds they hear around them
- learn that awareness of sound is a form of mindfulness practice

Materials
- instrument that reverberates with sound, such as a bell or a singing bowl, or a chiming alarm or sound on a smartphone (a six-second "Metal Gong" sound effect can be found at soundbible.com/tags-gong.html)

Mindful Check-In

Guide students through the Pause for a mindful check-in, referencing "Mindful Pauses to Begin and End Lessons" on page 17 for guidance as needed.

Activity

Explain: **Having courage means being ready to face whatever challenges come our way. By staying alert and aware of our surroundings, we can be more prepared. Today's exercise can also make you feel calmer and more present, which can be helpful when you're feeling anxious or fearful. One way to connect us to the present moment is to pay attention to the sounds around us. We often listen only to what we want to hear, even though there may be all sorts of different sounds around us. Listening to all of those different sounds is called using our Spidey Sense because it can give us an extra-sensitive awareness of our surroundings. We also call this awareness *mindfulness of sound*. Let's practice using our Spidey Sense.**

Bell/Chime Mindfulness
Ask students to find a comfortable seated position. If desired, they can close their eyes; otherwise, they can gaze downward. Prepare the instrument you will use to produce the sound (bell, singing bowl, chime on your phone).

Say: **I am going to ring this bell. Sit quietly and listen until the sound is completely gone. When you can no longer hear the sound, open your eyes and look at me.** Ring the bell.

Ask: **While you listened to the bell, were you able to stay focused in the present? Did you notice anything about your sense of hearing while you paid attention?** Discuss briefly.

Spidey Sense: Mindfulness of Sound

Ask: **Does anyone know what Spidey Sense Spider-Man has?** Elicit answers, pointing out that *Spidey Sense* refers to Spider-Man's super-sensitive, powerful senses. Review the five senses (sight, hearing, taste, smell, and touch).

Explain: **The next mindfulness activity can wake up our own Spidey Senses.** Ask students to sit comfortably with eyes closed or with a downward gaze. Follow the script below for guiding the activity, adapting as needed for your environment:

1. **Take a few deep belly breaths and let your body settle down.** Pause.

2. **Focus your attention on the sounds you hear around you.** Pause.

3. **See if you can pay attention to all the different sounds around you at once. Don't focus your attention on any one sound.** Pause.

4. **You may have thoughts that come into your mind. That's okay. Notice your thoughts, then come back to paying attention to sounds.**

5. **You may notice sounds coming from people near you or from outside. Or you may notice something in the classroom making a sound, like a clock or fan. Add that sound to your experience.** Pause.

6. **See if you can extend your sense of sound as far out as possible to include all the sounds around you.** Pause.

7. **You might also hear sounds inside of your body, like your heartbeat or your breathing. Notice these sounds too.** Pause.

8. Allow students another thirty seconds to one minute to practice.

Wrap-Up

Ask: **Did anyone notice their sense of hearing or other senses get stronger, like having Spidey Sense?** Elicit some answers.

Ask: **Do you think being alert like this makes you braver or more afraid?** Elicit some answers.

Explain: **We can focus our attention on what is happening around us—the sights, smells, and sounds. When we do this, our minds are in the present moment, not the future or past. This is a great way to practice mindfulness at any time. It also helps calm our bodies and our minds. In turn, this prepares us to face challenges that come our way and to take courageous actions, and it helps us stay mindful while we're dealing with those challenges.**

Mindful Checkout

Invite students to find a comfortable position and sit quietly. Choose one of these activities to guide your students through a mindful checkout, referencing "Mindful Pauses to Begin and End Lessons" on page 17 for guidance as needed:

- Practice the Pause
- Be Mindful of Change

Follow-Up

Throughout the week, you can practice shorter versions of this type of mindfulness of the senses. For example, before students return from recess, you can have them pause and pay attention to the sensations around them, like a breeze on their skin, the sounds around them, or anything they may see in nature.

LESSON 23
WHAT-IFS AND WHAT IS (COPE)

Lesson Summary
In this lesson, students will learn the nature of worries, called "what-ifs."

Keywords
- what-ifs
- what is
- worries

Students Will
- learn the nature of worries
- practice focusing on the present (what is) instead of worrying about the future (what-ifs)

Materials
- "What-Ifs and What Is" handout
- drawing supplies
- *for Worry Heroes activity variation*: "Worry Heroes" handout
- *for Worry Heroes activity variation*: art supplies (drawing and coloring utensils, colored paper, scissors, glue, yarn)

Mindful Check-In
Guide students through the Pause for a mindful check-in, referencing "Mindful Pauses to Begin and End Lessons" on page 17 for guidance as needed.

Activity

Ask: **What does it mean to worry?** Elicit a range of answers from students. Explain: **Worries are when we have fears about the worst *what-ifs*.**

On the whiteboard, write "What-Ifs." Ask students to share some what-ifs and write them down.

Select one of the what-ifs from the board as an example, or provide one of your own. For example, you could use "What if I don't finish my classwork on time?" Take the what-if example and add more and more what-ifs to it. You may choose to either write these on the board or say them out loud, depending on time. The intention is to show how these what-ifs can quickly pile up and become overwhelming.

Using the above example, your what-if sequence might look something like this:

"What if I don't finish my classwork on time?"

Then . . . "What if my teacher gets mad at me and yells at me in front of the class?"

And . . . "What if my teacher tells my parents?"

And . . . "What if my parents get mad at me?"

And . . . "What if they punish me for not doing my classwork?"

And . . . "What if I'm not allowed to go to the next grade?"

And . . . "What if I can never get into high school or college because I can't finish my work on time?"

Explain: **One of the problems with what-ifs is that they can grow and spread the more we pay attention to them. They are like weeds in a garden. Your first what-if worry can plant the seed for the next what-if, and soon your mind is full of a bunch of what-ifs.**

Divide students into pairs. Direct students to the "What-Ifs and What Is" handout. Say: **On the "What-Ifs" side, write down or draw pictures of the what-ifs that pop into your head. We often start with a "what-if," and then we add more and more bad things we imagine might happen. In the "And Then . . ." section, write down something that you worry might happen if the "what-if" actually occurs. Use your imagination and write or draw how big and overwhelming your what-ifs can get.**

Allow students three minutes to complete this part of the handout. Then, encourage students to share their what-ifs with their partner if they are comfortable sharing. Do not force students to share if they don't want to.

Explain: **In a way, these what-ifs are meant to protect us from what might happen. But our imaginations can come up with so many what-ifs that they can become a problem. Ask: What happens if we listen to our what-ifs all the time?** Elicit some answers.

Ask: **Does this help us be brave and face our fears, like trying new things or doing things that we get nervous about? Or do we want to stay away from doing these things when we listen to our what-ifs?** Discuss.

Direct students to the next section of the handout, titled "What Is."

Say: *What is* **means the way things are right now.** *What is* **means how things are in the present moment—not in the future, made-up world of what-ifs.**

Return to the example on the whiteboard. Add two more columns to the board and label them "What Is" and "What I Can Do Now."

In the "What Is" column, write down the concrete details related to *what is*. Using the previous example, you might write something like "What Is: I am doing my classwork now."

You can also add previous events to the "What Is" column that are opposite of the what-ifs:

In the same column, write (or say out loud): "Things that happened before that are the opposite of the what-ifs:" and make a list like this:

- I have finished my work most of the time.
- I have been able to ask my teacher for help.
- When I didn't finish all my work, I was allowed to finish it at home.
- I was able to ask my parents for help when I got stuck.
- Even when I didn't get it all done, it wasn't the end of the world.

Under the column "What I Can Do Now," write examples that are present-time focused, such as "I can focus on my work" and "I can ask for help."

Direct students to the two remaining sections of the worksheet. Say: **In the "What Is" section, draw or write what things are true *right now*, in the present moment.**

Say: **Then, after you finish with that, go to the section labeled "What I Can Do Now." Write anything down there that you can do now or very soon—not too far into the future. And try to use your positive problem-solving skills.** Allow students five minutes to complete this part.

Encourage students who are comfortable sharing to share their worksheets with their partners when they finish.

Wrap-Up

Say: **Our worries and what-ifs are things we imagine might happen. Many of these never do happen. A tiny bit of worry can get us to take action and prepare for the future, like when we're worried about finishing our homework, so we complete it and hand it in. But many times, our worries are the what-ifs that never happen. These fears can often keep us from facing challenges, trying new things, or meeting new people. The more often we can stay focused on the present moment—what *is*—the more courageous we can be to take on new challenges and opportunities.**

Mindful Checkout

Invite students to find a comfortable position and sit quietly. Choose one of these activities to guide your students through a mindful checkout, referencing "Mindful Pauses to Begin and End Lessons" on page 17 for guidance as needed:

- Practice the Pause
- Be Mindful of Change

Follow-Up

In the coming week, notice when students begin a statement with "What if. . . ." If it is a genuine question, like "What if we forgot our PE clothes today?" answer it normally. But if it sounds more like a worry type of what-if, then redirect the student by asking, "What is?" You can follow this up with the question, "What can you do now?" This simple reframing can help students remain in the present rather than add to their worries.

Variation
Worry Heroes

You can do this variation as an extension of the What-Ifs and What Is activity, or for younger students, you may do this variation instead of that activity.

1. Preparation: Make sure each student has a copy of the "Worry Heroes" handout. Provide each student with a pair of scissors and art supplies including things like colored paper, fabric, glue, and yarn.

2. Discuss the connection between what-ifs and worries if you haven't already (consult the instructions for

the What-Ifs and What Is activity above). Ask students to share some of their what-if worries.

3. Explain: **In some cultures, people make "worry dolls," which are meant to hold a person's worries. You can give your worries to the worry doll. At night, you put the worry doll under your pillow. And while you sleep, it will make your worries go away. You can use worry dolls as a place to put your worries so they don't bug you all day and night.** Explain that today, they are going to make Worry *Heroes* to do the same thing.

4. Ask students to cut out the Worry Hero on their worksheet. Offer additional copies of the worksheet if students want to create multiple Worry Heroes.

5. Invite them to color and decorate their Worry Hero(es) however they wish. You can suggest cutting out capes or making masks or hats.

6. Give students five to ten minutes to create their Worry Heroes.

7. Invite students to share their Worry Heroes with each other.

WHAT-IFS AND WHAT IS

What-Ifs

Under "What-If . . ." below, write down or draw the "what-ifs" that worry you. We often start with a "what-if," and then we imagine more and more bad things that might happen. In the "And Then . . ." section, write down something that you worry might happen if the "what-if" actually occurs.

What Is

Under "What Is," write or draw exactly what is happening *right now* related to your worry. After that, consider some of the things you can do now to help prevent or improve your "what-if" situation. Write those ideas under "What I Can Do Now."

What If . . .	And Then . . .	What Is:	What I Can Do Now:

Name:_____ Date:_____

From *Teaching Kids to Pause, Cope, and Connect: Lessons for Social-Emotional Learning and Mindfulness* by Mark Purcell, Psy.D., and Kellen Glinder, M.D., copyright © 2022. This page may be reproduced for individual, classroom, or small group work only. For other uses, contact Free Spirit Publishing at freespirit.com/permissions.

WORRY HEROES

Make your own Worry Hero using the instructions below.

1. Use different materials to dress up the figure below as your Worry Hero. You can use supplies like markers, glitter, paper cutouts, yarn, or cloth.

2. You can bring your Worry Hero home to keep with you when you face fears and worries.

Name:_____ Date:_____

From *Teaching Kids to Pause, Cope, and Connect: Lessons for Social-Emotional Learning and Mindfulness* by Mark Purcell, Psy.D., and Kellen Glinder, M.D., copyright © 2022. This page may be reproduced for individual, classroom, or small group work only. For other uses, contact Free Spirit Publishing at freespirit.com/permissions.

LESSON 24
FACE YOUR FEARS (CONNECT)

Lesson Summary

Students will take steps toward facing fears and asking for help in small-group role-playing.

Keywords

- facing fears
- asking for help

Students Will

- identify some of their fears
- role-play facing their fears
- give each other words of encouragement

Materials

- "Face My Fears" handout

Mindful Check-In

Guide students through the Pause for a mindful check-in, referencing "Mindful Pauses to Begin and End Lessons" on page 17 for guidance as needed.

Activity

Explain: **Our fears are connected to our worries and what-ifs. But we can take steps to face our fears. Our minds often tell us to run away from the things we fear. But when we do that, the fear grows in our minds.**

Ask for someone to share a fear, or provide an example, such as speaking or reading in front of the class.

Explain: **Our mind might tell us to stay away from doing the things we're afraid of. It can tell us that if we stay away, the fear will go away. And that could work in the moment. But does that really help us get over the fear?** Discuss with students.

Explain: **If we can learn to face our fears, bit by bit, they shrink instead of grow. We're going to do an activity to help each other face our fears.**

Demonstrate the Face Your Fears mini play. Ask for three volunteers. If a student who shared a fear is willing, they can be the star. Or you may pick any three students and use a fear example.

The three roles are (1) the Star, (2) the Fear, and (3) the Courage Coach. Assign each role to a student. Explain: **In this mini play, the Star is going to practice facing their Fear.** Direct attention to the student playing the Star and the one playing the Fear. **The Star will have the chance to call on a Courage Coach if they need help.** Indicate the student in the role of Courage Coach.

Ask the Star to tell their fear to the student playing the Fear. Then, the student playing the Fear should say: **I am your fear of [fear provided by the Star]. What are you going to do?**

Encourage the Star to come up with ideas of what they can do to face their Fear. Let the Star know that they can call up the Courage Coach to give ideas of what to say to the Fear. Provide guidance and direction as needed during the mini play. Allow the mini play to get silly or playful if that occurs. The lighthearted attitude toward the Fear will reduce anxiety.

Using the example of fear of speaking or reading in front of the class, the mini play might go something like this:

> Star: I am afraid of speaking in front of the class.
>
> Fear to Star: I am your fear of speaking in front of the class. What are you going to do?
>
> Star: I'm going to do it anyway. And I will try to take a deep breath first.
>
> *Star mimes being on a telephone and asks the Courage Coach for help.*
>
> Star: Courage Coach, how can I face my fear?
>
> Courage Coach: You can practice your speech with your friends first.
>
> Star to Fear: I'm going to practice with my friends.
>
> Star to Fear: I am going to face my fear and speak in front of class.

After the three actors have finished, applaud them. Ask the Star how they feel about their fear now.

Face Your Fears Activity

Divide students into groups of three. Direct them to the "Face Your Fears" handout. Invite them to write down some of their fears in the column labeled "I am

afraid of . . ." Give students two minutes to do this.

Guide the class through their mini plays using a script like the following:

1. Take turns playing the three roles—the Star, the Fear, and the Courage Coach.

2. **If you are playing the Star, pick one of your fears from the handout. Your job will be to face your fear and do something to help overcome it.**

3. **If you are playing the Fear, repeat back to the Star: "I am your fear of ____. What are you going to do?"**

4. **The Star should try to come up with anything they can to face the Fear. If the Star gets stuck, they can call the Courage Coach for help. The Courage Coach can cheer on the Star or suggest ways to face the Fear.**

5. Give students three minutes to role-play.

6. When the groups have finished the first round, ask the Star to write down any statements they said or that the Courage Coach said that helped them face the Fear. The students playing the Fear and the Courage Coach can help the Star remember if needed.

7. Ask groups to rotate the positions of the Star, the Fear, and the Courage Coach.

8. Allow groups two minutes to role-play on their own, and one minute for the Star to write down words of encouragement.

9. Ask groups to rotate the positions of the Star, the Fear, and the Courage Coach again.

10. Allow groups two minutes to role-play on their own and one minute for the Star to write down words of encouragement.

Wrap-Up

Ask: **How do each of you feel about your fears now? Are you more frightened or less?** Discuss.

Ask: **Did you learn new ways to face your fear?** Elicit examples. Explain: **Your fears will get weaker each time you try to face them instead of running from them. Next time you have the same fear, remember what you said today and tell that to yourself.**

Explain: **Sometimes we forget that the what-ifs cannot hurt us.** Place your hand on your heart and ask the students to do the same. Ask them to gently say, "I am safe. I am safe. I am safe." **Doing this can help you remember that you are safe and that you can face your fears.**

Mindful Checkout

Invite students to find a comfortable position and sit quietly. Choose one of these activities to guide your students through a mindful checkout, referencing "Mindful Pauses to Begin and End Lessons" on page 17 for guidance as needed:

- Practice the Pause
- Be Mindful of Change

Follow-Up

If you notice students worrying or saying what-ifs, you can remind them to focus on what *is*. You can encourage students to describe what is and what they can do now rather than focus on their what-ifs. Ask them to think of things they could say to their fears.

FACE MY FEARS

Write down or draw some of the things you are afraid of in the "I Am Afraid of . . ." column.

Next to it, write down some of the things you could say back to these fears.

Then, write down how saying those things to your fears makes you feel.

I Am Afraid of...	Something I Can Say to My Fear	This Makes Me Feel . . .
Example: I am afraid that someone is going to break into my house at night.	"My house is locked. My parents can protect me. No one has ever broken in before. I am safe."	Safer and calmer.

Name:_____ Date:_____

From *Teaching Kids to Pause, Cope, and Connect: Lessons for Social-Emotional Learning and Mindfulness* by Mark Purcell, Psy.D., and Kellen Glinder, M.D., copyright © 2022. This page may be reproduced for individual, classroom, or small group work only. For other uses, contact Free Spirit Publishing at freespirit.com/permissions.

LIFE SKILL IX
ACCEPT

*A*cceptance has dual meanings, both relevant to child development and mind-fulness. For one, *acceptance* is a positive and welcoming attitude about the strengths and limitations of ourselves and others. The second meaning refers to the acceptance of the world as it is (as opposed to resistance). This kind of acceptance can help children cope with the unexpected surprises and challenges in life.

The dynamics of acceptance and change are captured well by Reinhold Niebuhr's Serenity Prayer: "Grant me the serenity to accept the things I cannot change, the courage to change the things I can, and the wisdom to know the difference." As educators, one of the best skills we can teach young people is to develop their own wisdom to know this difference.

Many children have difficulties practicing self-acceptance and instead default to shame and blame. Modeling acceptance and unconditional positive regard promotes compassion toward the self and others and improves social-emotional health. Teacher-student relationships that are based on acceptance, affection, and empathy promote healthy psychological adjustment for both and foster a prosocial classroom environment. Self-acceptance influences the way young people look at the world and how they consider their own value and self-worth. It leads to resilience, emotional regulation, and a willingness to experience life and grow (Bernard et al. 2013).

Introducing This Life Skill to Students

There are different options for introducing the Accept life skill based on the needs of your group and your time limitations. The following lessons provide different learning experiences related to acceptance. If you are limited on time, you can start with the first lesson. Otherwise, you can introduce the skill with quotations and class discussion or by reading related books.

1. **Quotations and Socratic Questioning:** You may start a brief discussion by reading one of the quotations listed below (or another one chosen by you).

   - "If you are always trying to be normal, you will never know how amazing you can be." —Maya Angelou
   - "The things that make me different are the things that make me me." —Piglet in the film *Sing a Song with Pooh Bear*
   - "By being yourself you put something wonderful in the world that was not there before." —Edwin Elliott

   Follow up with questions such as:

   - What does this quotation mean to you?
   - How does it relate to acceptance?
   - Why do you think acceptance of yourself and others is an important life skill?
   - Can you share a time when you accepted yourself or someone else?

2. **Related Literature:** You may wish to connect this life skill to relevant children's literature. You can begin a lesson by reading one of the books listed below, or you can read parts of it between the three lessons related to this life skill.

   - *Giraffes Can't Dance* by Giles Andreae
   - *I Like Myself!* by Karen Beaumont
   - *I'm Gonna Like Me: Letting Off a Little Self-Esteem* by Jamie Lee Curtis

Further Resources

- "5 Tips for Teaching Your Kids Self-Compassion" by Margarita Tartakovsky, psychcentral.com/blog/5-tips-for-teaching-your-kids-self-compassion#1
- "Celebrating Differences: 5 Lessons for Teaching Kids Acceptance" by Chris Corsi, poehealth.org/celebrating-differences

LESSON 25
RAIN (PAUSE)

Lesson Summary

RAIN is a four-step mindfulness exercise designed to help students work through intense emotions. Students learn to simply recognize and accept strong feelings without reacting to them or pushing them away.

Keywords

- RAIN
- strong feelings

Students Will

- learn the four-step mindfulness practice RAIN: Recognize/notice, Allow, Investigate, Nurture/Non-identify ("Not me")
- practice noticing strong emotions without reacting to them

Materials

- "RAIN: Dealing with Strong Feelings" handout

Mindful Check-In

Guide students through the Pause for a mindful check-in, referencing "Mindful Pauses to Begin and End Lessons" on page 17 for guidance as needed.

Activity

Discuss how some feelings can feel more comfortable than others. Explain: **When we have uncomfortable feelings, we usually want to do one of two things: fix the feelings or push them away. But sometimes doing these things doesn't fix the problem and can even make things worse.**

Give a few brief examples of how trying to fix the feelings or pushing the feelings away can sometimes makes things worse, such as:

- You stub your toe, and your friend comes over to help. The pain from stubbing your toe makes you yell at your friend, so they leave. But the pain is still there, and now your friend is upset with you.

- You write an answer in the wrong place on a worksheet. This makes you angry, and the anger leads you to erase the answer very aggressively. This tears the paper, so you need to start over with a new worksheet.

- You're so excited that you know the answer in class that you end up talking over everyone else. It makes people feel like you don't care about their answers or what they have to say.

Next, work through the following scenarios as a class:

1. **If a girl is getting angry because her little sister keeps annoying her, what's something she might do to try and get rid of her anger?** Elicit problematic ways to "fix" her anger, like *She could hit her sister to make her stop.*

   Ask: **Is that a good way to "fix the feeling"? Or does it make it worse?** Discuss briefly.

2. **If a boy does badly on a spelling test and feels sad, what might he do to try to make his sadness go away?** Elicit problematic ways to "fix" his sadness like, *He could push the feeling away by throwing away the test and never thinking about it again.*

   Ask: **Is that a good way to "fix the feeling"? Or does it make it worse?** Discuss briefly.

You can also remind students of what they learned in the Have Courage life skill about facing fears instead of running away from them.

Say: **Remember, feelings are not good or bad. And they are always changing.** If you have the glitter jar from Lesson 1, you can shake it up and let students watch the glitter settle. Say: **If we notice what we're feeling, our feelings will usually settle down on their own. We can even learn something from those difficult feelings if we can let them be and use our Mindful Detective skills.**

RAIN Mindfulness Activity

The RAIN acronym is a method originally developed by meditation instructor Michele McDonald. For more information, see vipassanahawaii.org/resources/raindrop. Reprinted with permission.

Explain to students that they are going to do a mindfulness practice called RAIN. Write the four letters vertically on the whiteboard, followed by what each letter stands for:

R—Recognize

A—Allow (Let It Be)

I—Investigate (Mindful Detective)

N—Not Me and Nurture

Instruct students to find a comfortable position. Ask them to close their eyes or gaze downward. Begin by asking students to follow their breath for a few moments and quiet themselves.

Say: **For this mindfulness activity, we are going to try and notice a feeling that may be uncomfortable or unpleasant. In the quiet, explore your heart, body, and mind. Notice if there's a feeling that's troubling you. Or a body signal that feels uncomfortable. Or a thought that nags at you. Try to notice the feeling that comes with it.**

Pause for thirty seconds to one minute.

Say: **Now we are going to practice RAIN.** Reference the acronym on the board as you go through each step. **R:** *Recognize* **the feeling that you are having. Give the feeling a name if you can. Naming the feeling can take away its power over us.** Pause for thirty seconds to one minute.

A: *Allow* the feeling to be there, just as it is. It is most likely unpleasant, but it's just a feeling that will pass. It's here right now, so don't fight it. Don't try to fix it or push it away. Pause for thirty seconds to one minute.

I: *Investigate* the feeling. How does it feel in your body? Where are you feeling it most strongly? Pause. What types of thoughts does this feeling make you think about? Is it making you tense up or feel bad at all? Pause. Do you notice other feelings underneath this one? Pause.

N: *"Not Me"* (non-identification). Remind yourself that this feeling is not who you are; it's just a feeling that will go away with time. You may be feeling bad, but you are not bad. Sadness may be washing over you, but it will go away, and you don't have to hang on to it. It will pass. Pause.

N also stands for "nurture." Is there something this feeling is asking for, like a hug or acceptance? Or for you to feel proud or safe? Can you imagine giving that to yourself? Pause.

Encourage students to wrap their arms around themselves and give themselves a hug as they inhale deeply.

Say: **Be proud of yourself for caring for this hurt part of yourself.**

Wrap-Up

Explain that students can use RAIN whenever difficult feelings rise up inside. They may need to go through the whole RAIN process to work through the feelings, or they may just need to do one or two steps. Say: **The more experience you have working through each step, the easier it will be to understand what you need to do to work through the difficulty.**

Mindful Checkout

Invite students to find a comfortable position and sit quietly. Choose one of these activities to guide your students through a mindful checkout, referencing "Mindful Pauses to Begin and End Lessons" on page 17 for guidance as needed:

- Practice the Pause
- Be Mindful of Change

Follow-Up

In the next weeks, take notice when students seem to be feeling unpleasant or strong emotions. When you notice this, ask the student if they can practice RAIN. You may also want to have a designated quiet space where students can sit calmly to practice RAIN privately. This activity can also be very effective when done in one-on-one sessions you may have with the students or that students may have with a school counselor or psychologist.

RAIN: DEALING WITH STRONG FEELINGS

Use the RAIN skill to help you work through strong feelings. Follow the steps below to practice RAIN.

R: Recognize the feeling that you are having. Give the feeling a name if you can.

A: Allow the feeling to be there, just as it is. Don't fight it. Don't try to fix it or push it away.

I: Investigate the feeling. How does it feel in your body? Where are you feeling it most strongly? What types of thoughts does this feeling bring? Are you tensed up or feeling bad at all? Do you notice other feelings underneath this one?

N: "Not Me." Remind yourself that this feeling is not who you are; it's just a feeling that will go away with time. It will pass. N also stands for nurture. Is there something this feeling is asking for, like a hug or acceptance? Or for you to feel proud or safe? Can you imagine giving that to yourself?

Name:_____ Date:_____

From *Teaching Kids to Pause, Cope, and Connect: Lessons for Social-Emotional Learning and Mindfulness* by Mark Purcell, Psy.D., and Kellen Glinder, M.D., copyright © 2022. This page may be reproduced for individual, classroom, or small group work only. For other uses, contact Free Spirit Publishing at freespirit.com/permissions.

LESSON 26
CARING FOR FEELINGS (COPE)

Lesson Summary
Students will identify some of the uncomfortable feelings they sometimes have and things they can do to move toward more positive feelings.

Keywords
- feeling zones
- improving mood

Students Will
- identify difficult feelings they have, as well as the thoughts and body signals that go with them
- consider things they can do to help themselves feel better
- identify who can help them when they have difficult feelings

Materials
- "Caring for My Feelings" handout
- "All the Things I Can Do" handout
- "How Are You Feeling?" handout (from Feelings Charades activity in Lesson 18)

Preparation
Copy the prompts under "Caring for This Feeling" from the "Caring for My Feelings" handout onto the whiteboard.

Mindful Check-In
Guide students through the Pause for a mindful check-in, referencing "Mindful Pauses to Begin and End Lessons" on page 17 for guidance as needed.

Activity
Explain that when we learn to accept our feelings, it is easier to take care of them. Say: **What you do to care for your feelings will depend on who you are and what the feeling is.**

Ask: **Does anyone remember the four feeling zones?** Elicit answers. **Sometimes, there are different ways to care for feelings in different feeling zones.** Give a few examples.

- Angry Zone: **If you're feeling angry, you may need to go run around outside to get that energy out and get the volume of your feeling to go down.**
- Sad Zone: **If you're feeling sad, it may help to talk to someone about it.**
- Scared Zone: **If you're feeling scared, you may want to try to face your fear.**

Tell students they are going to investigate some of those difficult feelings. They are also going to think of things they can do to care for those feelings.

FIGURE 6: CARING FOR MY FEELINGS SAMPLE

Caring for Feelings Script	Example
When I feel _____ . . .	When I feel <u>ANGRY</u> . . .
In my body I feel _____,	In my body I feel <u>tense muscles, heat on my face</u>.
I think to myself _____,	I think to myself <u>I want to scream, I'm so frustrated and mad.</u>
To care for (or change) that feeling, I can . . .	To care for (or change) that feeling I can . . .
do (at school): _____,	do (at school): <u>walk away, take a few deep breaths, go to the bathroom and splash water on my face.</u>
do (at home): _____,	do (at home): <u>go to my room and listen to music, draw, or build with LEGO bricks; pet my dog.</u>
To ask for help, I can say _____,	To ask for help, I can say: <u>"I'm getting upset. I feel frustrated."</u>
People I can ask: _____	People I can ask: <u>My teacher, my parents.</u>

Caring for My Feelings Activity

Divide students into groups of three. Distribute the "Caring for My Feelings," "All the Things I Can Do," and "How Are You Feeling?" handouts. Instruct them to take out the "Caring for My Feelings" handout. Using the prompts copied onto the whiteboard, go through the example in figure 6 above.

Walk students through each of the prompts, giving examples and answering questions as needed. For the first prompt ("When I feel . . ."), explain that each of them may have a different feeling that is difficult for them or that causes them problems when it is too strong. Say:

Think about what that feeling is for you. Ask: **What are the body signals you get when you are having that feeling? What are the thoughts that go with that feeling? Write those down or draw a picture. Remember to describe as much as you can.**

Allow students three minutes to complete this first prompt.

Direct students to the second prompt, "To care for (or change) that feeling, I can . . ." Explain: **There are many things we can do to take care of a difficult feeling. What we can do at school may be different than what we can do at home. List as many activities as you can think of that could help you take care of that**

feeling. If you need ideas, look at the "All the Things I Can Do" handout or ask for suggestions from the people in your group.

Allow students five to seven minutes to complete this section.

Direct students to the third prompt ("To ask for help, I can say . . .") and say: **Next, think of what you can say to someone to get help. What would help you take care of that feeling so you can feel better? Write down what you could say. Then write down who you could ask for help.** Examples:

- "I'm getting really frustrated. Can you help me?" (Ask your teacher.)

- "My feelings were hurt when . . ." (Tell a friend or parent.)

- "The loud noises are bothering me. Can I go someplace quieter?" (Ask your teacher or parent.)

Allow two minutes to complete this section.

If time allows, ask each student to practice saying the phrase they wrote down to another member in their group.

Wrap-Up

Explain: **The Pause can be very helpful when you have difficult feelings. First, you can use your breath to keep the difficult feeling from becoming too big. Then, you can notice your thoughts and body signals so you can name the feeling. Finally, you can make a wise decision about what to do to care for that feeling.**

Encourage students to save their "Caring for My Feelings" handouts, or collect them and keep them for the next lesson, Sharing Feelings.

Mindful Checkout

Invite students to find a comfortable position and sit quietly. Choose one of these activities to guide your students through a mindful checkout, referencing "Mindful Pauses to Begin and End Lessons" on page 17 for guidance as needed:

- Practice the Pause
- Be Mindful of Change

Follow-Up

During the following week, provide students with extra copies of the "Caring for My Feelings" handout. Encourage students to identify other challenging feelings as they arise in the following days and weeks. When you notice challenging feelings arise, remind students of some of the things they can do to care for those feelings.

CARING FOR MY FEELINGS

Circle one of the feelings below that is difficult for you to feel, or choose one that causes problems for you when it gets too strong. You can also circle a picture from the "How Are You Feeling?" chart or draw an emoji. Then try to answer each of the prompts under "Caring for This Feeling."

Feeling Zones

Feeling Zone	Feelings						
Happy/ Peaceful	Happy	Silly	Giggly	Hyper	Hysterical	Joyful	Cheery
	Content	Relaxed	Calm				
Angry	Angry	Annoyed	Bothered	Raging	Furious	Stubborn	Arguing
	Complaining	Rebellious	Defiant	Defensive			
Sad	Sad	Lonely	Down	Tearful	Negative	Hopeless	Tired
	Lazy	Weak	Exhausted				
Scared	Frightened	Worried	Nervous	Anxious	Restless	Guarded	Scared
	Terrified						

Caring for This Feeling

When I feel _____ . . .

In my body I feel _____,

I think to myself _____,

To care for (or change) that feeling, I can . . .

do (at school) _____

_____,

do (at home) _____

_____,

To ask for help, I can say _____,

People I can ask: _____

Name:_____ Date:_____

From *Teaching Kids to Pause, Cope, and Connect: Lessons for Social-Emotional Learning and Mindfulness* by Mark Purcell, Psy.D., and Kellen Glinder, M.D., copyright © 2022. This page may be reproduced for individual, classroom, or small group work only. For other uses, contact Free Spirit Publishing at freespirit.com/permissions.

All the Things I Can Do

There are many things you can do to take care of a difficult feeling. What you can do at school may be different from what you can do at home. Here are some ideas.

Physical	Walk	Run	Play a Sport	Dance	Yoga
	Ride Bike	Play Tag	Jungle Gym	Build	Garden
	Exercise				
Quiet and Relaxing	Read	Do Puzzles	Code		
	Take a Hot Bath	Use Scented Oils	Ask for Shoulder Massage	Sleep/Nap	Yoga
Social	Play Board Games	Call a Friend	Play Online Games		Camp
	Video Call	Go to Park with Friend	Walk with Friend	Visit Family	Bike Ride with Friend
	Help Out	Do Role-Playing Games	Play with Pets		
Creative	Write	Draw	Play Music	Paint	Invent
	Build	Play *Minecraft*	Sew	Make a Collage	Dance
	Listen to Music		Do Crafts		

Name:_____ Date:_____

From *Teaching Kids to Pause, Cope, and Connect: Lessons for Social-Emotional Learning and Mindfulness* by Mark Purcell, Psy.D., and Kellen Glinder, M.D., copyright © 2022. This page may be reproduced for individual, classroom, or small group work only. For other uses, contact Free Spirit Publishing at freespirit.com/permissions.

LESSON 27
SHARING FEELINGS (CONNECT)

Lesson Summary

In this lesson, students will share a difficult feeling and name something they can do to care for that feeling to move into a healthier feeling zone.

Keywords

- caring for difficult feelings
- feeling zones

Students Will

- identify difficult feelings they may experience
- identify ways to care for those feelings
- learn how to move into more peaceful feeling zones

Materials

- the completed "Caring for My Feelings" handouts from the previous lesson (Caring for Feelings)

Preparation

Arrange an empty space in the classroom that is near either the whiteboard or a flip chart with paper. On the board or chart paper, write "Happy/Peaceful Zone."

Mindful Check-In

Guide students through the Pause for a mindful check-in, referencing "Mindful Pauses to Begin and End Lessons" on page 17 for guidance as needed.

Activity

Explain: **You've all been working on noticing and investigating the difficult feelings you have and thinking up things you can do to care for them. Today, we're going to share what we've learned about our feelings so we can work together to build a more peaceful classroom community.**

Note: Remind everyone of their community commitments, as some students may feel vulnerable sharing some of these experiences.

Caring for Difficult Feelings Activity

Depending on your preference and classroom space, instruct students to either remain at their desks or tables, or to stand in a line in a section of the classroom. Direct their attention to the area you have marked as the Happy/Peaceful Zone.

Explain: **Each of us is going to take a turn naming a feeling that is difficult for us. You can also choose to describe how it feels in your body or a thought you have with it. But you don't have to. Then, we're going to describe what we can do to care for that feeling or what we can do to change it, so we**

don't do something we feel bad about later. I'll start.

1. Pick a difficult feeling you may experience and name it. You may say something like, "I have a hard time feeling . . ." or "It makes me uncomfortable to feel . . ."

2. Describe how it feels in your body and any thoughts that come up when you have it.

3. Then describe something you do to care for that feeling (you can name more than one). Then walk across the room to the area marked as the Happy/Peaceful Zone.

4. Write the feeling on the whiteboard or flip chart, then draw an arrow pointing to the right. On the right side of the arrow, write down what you do to care for the feeling.

5. Wave back to the rest of the students and ask, "Who's next?"

6. One by one, students name a difficult feeling they have.

7. You can ask each student to describe the body signals they get or the thoughts that sometimes come up when their feeling is happening, but they don't have to do this step if they don't want to.

8. Ask each student to name something they can do to care for that feeling.

9. Then have them walk over to the Happy/Peaceful Zone.

10. Older students can write the feeling and caring action on the whiteboard when they reach the Happy/Peaceful Zone. For younger students, you may choose to write the feeling and caring action on the board. *Note: It's okay if you don't have the time to record all the feelings and caring actions. The*

shared experience for the students is more important. But if you have time for it, this provides some visual reinforcement.

11. Be sure to praise students for sharing their difficult feelings. Welcome them with enthusiasm as they arrive to the Happy/Peaceful Zone. This will help the students who have not shared feel encouraged to join the others in the Happy/Peaceful Zone.

Note: If there are any students who feel too shy or guarded to share, you can ask them to get their paper from the previous lesson. Those students can either read aloud from the worksheet if that helps, or they can privately show it to you and move over to the Happy/Peaceful Zone without sharing. Be sure to encourage these students as well. You can even use this as an opportunity to point out that we can all feel very sensitive about our difficult feelings, so we should be extra kind and respectful to others when they are dealing with them.

When the entire class has reached the Happy/Peaceful Zone, ask them to stop and practice the Pause. Say: **Notice how we all feel right now. What would our class feel like if we were all caring for our feelings in this way, all at the same time?** Pause.

Direct students to the whiteboard or flip chart where you wrote down the difficult feelings and caring actions. Ask: **Remember the Big Feelings list we wrote a few weeks ago? The feelings on the board were all jumbled together with behaviors related to those feelings.** Discuss the differences between that list and the new list you've created.

Ask: **What's the difference between doing an activity to *get rid* of Big Feelings and doing an activity to *take care* of those feelings?** Discuss.

Ask: **How do you think mindfulness relates to this lesson?** Discuss.

Wrap-Up

Explain the importance of continuing to stop and notice what we are experiencing and to practice the Pause. Say: **If you notice you're dealing with a difficult feeling, try to do one of these actions to care for that feeling. If you see another classmate having a hard time, you might suggest trying one of these caring actions. This way, we can try to create a classroom community where we help each other through difficult feelings instead of passing those tough feelings back and forth to each other.**

Mindful Checkout

Invite students to find a comfortable position and sit quietly. Choose one of these activities to guide your students through a mindful checkout, referencing "Mindful Pauses to Begin and End Lessons" on page 17 for guidance as needed:

- Practice the Pause
- Be Mindful of Change

Follow-Up

During the next week, you may choose to keep the Happy/Peaceful Zone up in your classroom. When you notice a student struggling, you can ask them to do the Pause and consider what they might do to get to the Happy/Peaceful Zone.

Considerations

It is possible that students may bring up feelings and thoughts related to situations that are too personal or intense for the classroom setting. For example, children who have experienced trauma may bring up very scary or upsetting experiences. If you are concerned this may be the case for students in your class, you can set guidelines before doing the activity. Prior to the activity, you might say, "Now, we are going to try not to share feelings or experiences that might be scary for other students or that are private. I may tell you that what you are sharing is a little too personal. If that happens, we can talk about your experience privately after the lesson." This way, students do not feel rejected after sharing material that is too personal. Our experience has been that students are very good about respecting these boundaries, especially if they are stated beforehand. If students share concerning feelings or experiences, provide them with the support to speak to the school counselor or psychologist.

LIFE SKILL X
BE KIND

Kindness can literally change the brain. Acts of kindness have been shown to release serotonin, a neurotransmitter that plays a role in learning, memory, sleep, and mood. Kindness and mindfulness practices focused on compassion and empathy have also been shown to reduce levels of cortisol, the body's stress hormone (Engert et al. 2017). Practicing kindness has been shown to improve peer acceptance and self-esteem in children (Layous et al. 2012). People who feel depressed or anxious tend to have a type of tunnel vision, directing fears and negativity toward themselves. Acts of kindness can help people direct their attention outward to others.

School is where children practice many of the social skills that will guide them throughout their development. Teaching them to practice kindness improves their social-emotional well-being, self-esteem, and physical health.

Introducing This Life Skill to Students

There are different options for introducing the Be Kind life skill to students based on the needs of your group and your time limitations. The following lessons provide learning experiences related to kindness. If you are limited on time, you can start with the first lesson. Otherwise, you can introduce the skill with quotations and class discussion or by reading related books.

1. **Quotations and Socratic Questioning:** You may start a brief discussion by reading one of the quotations listed below (or another one chosen by you).

   - "We rise by [lifting] others." —Robert Ingersoll

   - "No act of kindness, no matter how small, is ever wasted." —Adapted from Aesop

   - "The simple act of caring is heroic." —Edward Albert

- "When you are kind to others, it not only changes you—it changes the world." —Harold Kushner

- "I've learned that people will forget what you said. People will forget what you did. But people will never forget how you made them feel." —Adapted from Carl Buehner

Follow up your chosen quotation with questions such as:

- What does this quotation mean to you?

- How does it relate to kindness?

- Why do you think that Be Kind is an important life skill?

- Can you share a time you used were kind?

2. **Related Literature:** You may wish to connect this life skill to relevant children's literature. You can begin a lesson by reading one of the books listed below, or you can read parts of it between the three lessons related to this life skill.

   - *The Invisible String* by Patrice Karst

   - *I Am Human: A Book of Empathy* by Susan Verde

Further Resources

- "7 Reasons Why Teaching Children Kindness Is Essential" by Marine Corps Community Services, usmc-mccs.org/articles/7-reasons-why-teaching-children-kindness-is-essential

- "Why Teaching Kindness in Schools Is Essential to Reduce Bullying" by Lisa Currie, edutopia.org/blog/teaching-kindness-essential-reduce-bullying-lisa-currie

LESSON 28
GROWING KINDNESS (PAUSE)

Lesson Summary
Students will draw pictures of people who make them feel special, then follow a mindfulness visualization of extending feelings of well-being to these individuals. (This is also known as a loving-kindness mindfulness practice.)

Keywords
- visualization
- gratitude
- kindness

Students Will
- identify their social supports
- learn a mindfulness practice to extend kindness to others

Materials
- "Growing Kindness" handout

Mindful Check-In
Guide students through the Pause for a mindful check-in, referencing "Mindful Pauses to Begin and End Lessons" on page 17 for guidance as needed.

Activity
Explain: **Kindness is both an action and a type of feeling. When others are kind to us, we feel good inside.** Ask students to share a time someone was kind to them. Say: **When we're kind to others, we also feel good about ourselves inside.** Ask students to share a time they were kind to someone else and how that felt.

Explain: **Bad feelings and unkindness can spread. When someone is unkind to us, we feel bad about ourselves. And sometimes, we pass that unkindness on to someone else.** Ask: **Can anyone think of a time someone was unkind to you, and then you felt bad and passed the unkindness on to someone else?** Elicit an example or two.

Explain: **That's why it is important to try to choose kindness. That way, we can feel the good feeling that comes with being kind. And just as bad feelings can spread, kindness can spread to others too. Then they can pass it on to others, who can pass it on to others, and on and on.**

Growing Kindness Activity
Give students copies of the "Growing Kindness" handout. Tell them that they will spend about two minutes drawing in each of the four areas of the worksheet.

Have them start in the first area by drawing a picture of someone who makes them feel special. Explain: **This can be just about anyone in your life—such as a parent, a grandparent, a friend, or**

a teacher. **It should be someone who makes you feel good about yourself, extra special. This can even be someone who's no longer living.** If they choose to, students can write down how they feel/felt around that person.

Then, have students move on to the next area of the handout, where they can draw people who they are close to, like friends or family members. It can be one person or a few. Encourage students to draw fun or pleasant activities they may do with those people.

Next, have them draw pictures for the classes or special groups. Say: **Draw a group of people you know, but maybe not as well as your family or closest friends. These may be the people in your class, teammates in a sport you play, or kids from a club you're in.**

Last, have students draw a picture of their community. Allow them the freedom to choose the community they want to draw. Say: **If you are part of a religious group or another special community, you may draw them. You could draw people from your neighborhood or from our school. Or you could draw people from your larger family who may live farther away. You can also draw people who have passed away and are no longer living.** The intention of the drawing activity is to have students focus on expanding their circle of connection and kindness.

Note: It is best for students to shift directly from the drawing activity into the mindfulness activity without discussion or sharing. This allows them to focus attention on the feelings that came during the drawing process.

Mindful Kindness Activity

Instruct students to get into a comfortable position. Ask them to spend a few moments looking at the pictures on their "Growing Kindness" handouts. Lead them through the Pause while they absorb their pictures. Have them breathe with awareness, then notice (1) body sensations, (2) thoughts, and (3) feelings.

Instruct students to close their eyes or gaze downward. Guide them through the Growing Kindness mindfulness activity:

1. **First, think of the first person you drew, the person who makes you feel special. Try to create a clear image of that person in your mind.** Pause for a few moments.

2. **Now, try to remember how you feel when you are around that person. Try to really let that feeling grow in your body and heart. You can even imagine a spot of warm light growing in your chest.** Pause for about thirty seconds.

3. **In your mind, thank that person for everything they have done for you. Imagine that warm light of kindness inside you spreading outward to touch that person.**

4. **In your inner voice, make a wish for them to be happy, safe, and free from difficulties.** Pause for a few moments.

5. **Next, think of the person or people who are close to you that you drew. This may be your family or friends. You can think of one person or a small group. Create a clear image of these people in your mind.** Pause for a few moments.

6. **Now, imagine how you feel when you are around those people. You might have some mixed feelings— some good and others uncomfortable. That's okay. If you can, try to focus on the happier, more pleasant times with those people. Try to let those good feelings grow in your body and heart. Imagine that warm light spreading through your body.** Pause for about fifteen seconds.

7. **Now, imagine that warm light of kindness spreading outward to those people.**

8. **In your inner voice, make a wish for them to be happy, safe, and free from difficulties.** Pause for a few moments.

9. **Next, imagine the people you know from a particular group. You may have drawn people from a sports team, from a club, or even from our class. Try to get a clear image of these people in your mind.** Pause for a few moments.

10. **Now, imagine how you feel when you are around those people. Again, you may have mixed feelings. But try to focus on the happier, more pleasant times. Let that warm, light feeling grow in your body and heart.** Pause.

11. **Now, imagine that warm light of kindness spreading outward to those people.** Pause for about fifteen seconds.

12. **In your inner voice, make a wish for them to be happy, safe, and free from difficulties.** Pause for a few moments.

13. **Next, imagine your warm light of kindness spreading out even farther. Think about the last group of people you drew, the people who live in your neighborhood or community.**

14. **Imagine how you feel around those people or in that community. Let that feeling of warm light grow in your body and heart.** Pause for about fifteen seconds.

15. **Now, imagine that warm glow of kindness spreading outward to those people.**

16. **In your inner voice, make a wish for them to be happy, safe, and free from difficulties.** Pause for a few moments.

17. **Imagine that warm glow of kindness growing each time you breathe in. As you breathe out, imagine it spreading farther and farther. See how far it can go. Let it spread out throughout your town, your city. Let it spread out into nature and all around the world. Breathe in peace.** Breathe in. **Breathe out kindness.** Breathe out. Pause for fifteen seconds.

18. **In your inner voice, make a wish for all people and living creatures to be happy, safe, and free from difficulties.** Pause.

19. **Finally, bring that glowing light of kindness back inside your body. Let it spread all the way through you.**

20. **On your next breath, say to yourself,** *May I be happy.* Give students a moment to take a breath. **On the next breath, say to yourself,** *May I be safe.* Give students another moment to take a breath. **And on the next**

breath, say to yourself, *May I be free from difficulty.* Pause for about fifteen seconds.

21. Ask students to gradually open their eyes, then stretch and wiggle their bodies.

Ask students to share how that mindfulness activity felt for them. Try to get them to describe how it felt both physically and emotionally. Ask: **How did it feel to imagine being around these special people in our lives?** Ask a few students to share some of the people they drew pictures of and how those people make them feel. Ask: **How did it feel to imagine sending kind feelings and wishes to these people?** Elicit responses.

Wrap-Up

Explain: **Kindness is both a feeling and an action. When we extend kindness to others, it makes us feel good, just as we feel better when others show us kindness. If we try, we can create a lot of kindness and goodwill for ourselves and others.**

Mindful Checkout

Invite students to find a comfortable position and sit quietly. Choose one of these activities to guide your students through a mindful checkout, referencing "Mindful Pauses to Begin and End Lessons" on page 17 for guidance as needed:

- Practice the Pause
- Be Mindful of Change

Follow-Up

You may choose to hang the "Growing Kindness" drawings the class made. During the following week, you may repeat this mindfulness activity. You can suggest that students imagine different people each time as they extend their circles of kindness.

Variation
The Invisible String

This lesson goes very well with the book *The Invisible String* by Patrice Karst. The book describes an invisible string of love that reaches from heart to heart and binds us all. If you like, you can read that book either before or after this lesson. After you finish both, link the book's theme with the mindfulness practice in class discussion.

Growing Kindness

In the spaces below, draw pictures of the people in your life who make you feel good when you are around them. If you want, you may also write about how they make you feel.

Someone Who Makes Me Feel Special	**My Family or Friends**
How I feel around this person:	How I feel around these people:
My Class or Special Groups (sports, arts, clubs, etc.)	**My School, Neighborhood, or Community** (extended family, religious community, etc.)
How I feel around these people:	How I feel around these people:

Name:_____   Date:_____

From *Teaching Kids to Pause, Cope, and Connect: Lessons for Social-Emotional Learning and Mindfulness* by Mark Purcell, Psy.D., and Kellen Glinder, M.D., copyright © 2022. This page may be reproduced for individual, classroom, or small group work only. For other uses, contact Free Spirit Publishing at freespirit.com/permissions.

LESSON 29
SELF-PORTRAIT AND SELF-ACCEPTANCE (COPE)

Lesson Summary

Students identify personal strengths and challenges, then complete a self-portrait that features the helpers in their lives.

Keywords

- self-portrait
- self-acceptance
- strengths and challenges
- helpers

Students Will

- identify their strengths, challenges, and social supports
- draw a self-portrait with their social supports

Materials

- "My Self-Portrait" handout
- "All About Me" handout
- drawing supplies

Note: If possible, print the two handouts on opposite sides of the same sheet of paper or staple them together.

Mindful Check-In

Guide students through the Pause for a mindful check-in, referencing "Mindful Pauses to Begin and End Lessons" on page 17 for guidance as needed.

Activity

After practicing the Pause, ask students to notice their body signals and feelings as you follow this script:

Firmly say **No.** Pause. Repeat: **No.** Pause. Say **No** one more time. Say: **Notice how you feel inside. What kind of signals is your body sending?** Pause.

Say: **Now listen to me.** In an encouraging voice, say **Yes** three times, pausing after each time.

Ask: **Did you notice a difference in how those statements made you feel?** Elicit responses.

Next, do the same with the following phrases.

In a scolding voice, say: **You should.** Pause. Say: **You shouldn't.** Repeat two more times, pausing between statements.

Ask students to notice how they feel inside.

Then, with enthusiasm, say: **You can.** Pause. Repeat two more times, pausing between statements.

Discuss the differences students felt between the statements.

Explain: **The words we hear over and over can turn into the words we tell ourselves. When we hear "No," "You should," or "You shouldn't" a lot, it**

becomes hard to like ourselves just the way we are.

Say: **Today we are going to practice self-acceptance.** Ask: **What do you think that means?** Elicit some answers. **Self-acceptance means liking yourself just the way you are.**

Self-Portrait Activity

1. Ask students to take out the "All About Me" handout.

2. Explain: **First, think about your strengths and superpowers, the things you like about yourself and the qualities you have that you are proud of.**

3. Instruct students to write down these strengths or draw pictures of them on the worksheet. Allow students two minutes to complete this.

4. Say: **Next, think of things that are hard for you. Just as every superhero has a weakness, you each have things you struggle with. It's important to accept and care for those parts of yourself too.**

5. Instruct students to write down these things that challenge them or draw pictures of them on the worksheet. Allow students two minutes to complete this.

6. Explain: **We all have people in our lives who help us out and make us feel special. These may be the same people you drew in the last lesson. Imagine these people and the ways they support you. Think of them as your Hero Helpers.**

7. Instruct students to write down the names of their Hero Helpers or draw pictures of them on the worksheet. Allow students two minutes to complete this.

8. When students have finished the worksheet, ask them to move to the "My Self-Portrait" handout.

9. Direct students to the oval frame in the center. Say: **In the oval, draw a picture of yourself. Use your imagination. Include your strengths and your challenges. Add colors, images, and symbols that are important to you. Show as much of who you are as you can in your self-portrait.**

10. Direct students to the area around the portrait frame. Say: **In the area around your portrait, draw the people and places that make you feel special. Again, use your imagination. Include as much as you can of your world of social support.**

11. Allow students six to eight minutes to complete their self-portraits.

Wrap-Up

When students have finished, ask them to look at their self-portraits. Say: **In the last lesson, we imagined sending feelings of friendliness and kindness to the people around us. We have to be kind to ourselves too. As you look at your self-portrait, imagine a feeling of kindness and warmth growing inside.** Invite everyone to place a hand over their heart. Say: **As you breathe in, tell yourself in your mind, "I accept me." As you breathe out, tell yourself in your mind, "Just the way I am."** Allow students to focus their attention this way for one minute.

Mindful Checkout

Invite students to find a comfortable position and sit quietly. Choose one of these activities to guide your students through a mindful checkout, referencing "Mindful Pauses to Begin and End Lessons" on page 17 for guidance as needed:

- Practice the Pause
- Be Mindful of Change

Follow-Up

Ask students to keep their self-portraits and "All About Me" handouts for the next lesson. Tell students that they can continue to add to their self-portraits throughout the week if they like.

MY SELF-PORTRAIT

- Self-Portrait: Draw a picture of yourself in the oval frame. Use your imagination. Add any colors, symbols, or images that show special things about you. Inside the frame, around the picture of you, write or draw your superhero strengths.
- Hero Helpers: In the space around your self-portrait, draw your Hero Helpers or write their names.

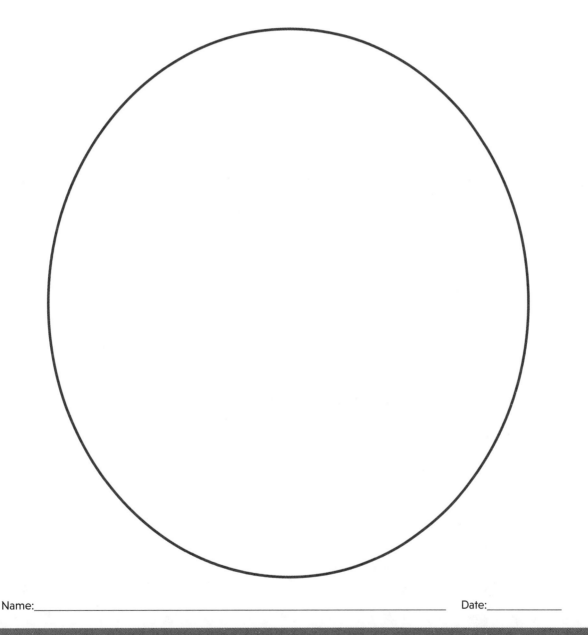

Name:_____ Date:_____

From *Teaching Kids to Pause, Cope, and Connect: Lessons for Social-Emotional Learning and Mindfulness* by Mark Purcell, Psy.D., and Kellen Glinder, M.D., copyright © 2022. This page may be reproduced for individual, classroom, or small group work only. For other uses, contact Free Spirit Publishing at freespirit.com/permissions.

ALL ABOUT ME

Take some time to think about the questions below. You can respond to each question by writing your answers or by drawing pictures of your answers.

We all have superpowers and strengths—things that we're good at or proud of. What are your superpowers or strengths?

My superpowers/strengths are . . .

We all have things that are hard or challenging for us and things we want to work on. What are your challenges?

My challenges are . . .

Who are some people in your life who make you feel special and support you?

My Hero Helpers are . . .

Name:_____ Date:_____

From *Teaching Kids to Pause, Cope, and Connect: Lessons for Social-Emotional Learning and Mindfulness* by Mark Purcell, Psy.D., and Kellen Glinder, M.D., copyright © 2022. This page may be reproduced for individual, classroom, or small group work only. For other uses, contact Free Spirit Publishing at freespirit.com/permissions.

LESSON 30
KIND COMMUNITY (CONNECT)

Lesson Summary

Students will share their self-portraits with one another in small groups. Then, they will learn about how kindness and acceptance lead to a healthy community.

Keywords

- kindness
- acceptance
- community

Students Will

- share how they view themselves
- practice acceptance of each other
- learn the importance of kindness in a healthy community

Materials

- Completed "Self Portrait" handouts from Lesson 29
- Completed "All About Me" handouts from Lesson 29
- *optional*: Three Cs of Community posters from Lesson 3, if available

Preparation

If you have them, display the Three Cs of Community posters that were created during Lesson 3.

Fill out blank copies of the "My Self-Portrait" and "All About Me" handouts with your own pictures and answers to the questions.

Mindful Check-In

Guide students through the Pause for a mindful check-in, referencing "Mindful Pauses to Begin and End Lessons" on page 17 for guidance as needed.

Activity

Remind students of the three Cs of community (caring, connecting, and contributing). If you have the posters, direct students' attention to them. Ask students to share ways that they have done each of the Cs in the past weeks and months. Ask: **Have these acts of kindness toward one another made us stronger and happier as a community? How?**

Explain: **Next, we are going to practice kindness and acceptance of each other as a community.**

Circle of Understanding Activity

Divide students into groups of about six to eight. Ask each group to form a circle.

Instruct students to hold their self-portraits in front them. *Note: If you have a smaller class size, or if time allows, you may choose to do this with the entire class.*

Explain: **I want each of you to take a turn presenting your self-portrait and sharing your strengths, challenges, and Hero Helpers. When it's your turn, hold**

your self-portrait up for the rest of the group to see. Then read your answers to the questions on the "All About Me" worksheet.

Hold up your own self-portrait as a demonstration. Say: **I am (your name).** Follow this by sharing your responses to the prompts on the "All About Me" worksheet.

Ask: **Did I miss any superpowers or strengths about me?** Wait for some answers. This may feel slightly uncomfortable, but it's important to demonstrate being comfortable with others giving you compliments or identifying your strengths. You may even share how that felt to you.

Say: **After you have shared your self-portrait, the other people in your group should add to your strengths and superpowers. At least one person from the group needs to name an extra superpower strength before you move on to the next person.**

Allow students ten minutes to complete this activity. Circle the room to provide guidance and encouragement.

Wrap-Up

When they have finished, ask students to form a larger circle with the whole class. Ask everyone to hold up their self-portraits. Encourage them to take a few minutes looking around the room at the different self-portraits. Ask: **Do all these pictures look the same? Or is each one unique?** Ask students to define the word *unique*, or provide your own definition. Say: **Our differences are what make us special. We all have unique gifts and talents.** Ask students to share something

positive or kind that they learned about one of their classmates. Say: **We all have a special place and purpose in the world. Let's keep supporting each other with kindness and understanding.**

Mindful Checkout

Invite students to find a comfortable position and sit quietly. Choose one of these activities to guide your students through a mindful checkout, referencing "Mindful Pauses to Begin and End Lessons" on page 17 for guidance as needed:

- Practice the Pause
- Be Mindful of Change

For this final mindful checkout, you may choose to do the **Be Mindful of Change** checkout, as it relates to the entire Pause, Cope, and Connect program.

Follow-Up

You can hang students' self-portraits up in the room. Check to make sure each student feels comfortable having this personal portrait posted. You can also do a follow-up activity of adding more to the Three Cs of Community posters. If you have the original posters, you can add to them, or you can have the students make new posters. When finished, you may choose to hang those posters up in the classroom as well.

During the weeks that follow, you can pick and choose lessons and activities from this book to repeat based on the current needs of your class. This will support mastery of the skills, and most of these activities will yield different outcomes and insights each time they are done.

RESOURCES

Picture Books
Body Awareness, Feelings, and SEL

My Incredible Talking Body: Learning to be Calm by Rebecca Bowen, illustrated by Lauren Bowen (2017). This is a book that helps children learn to recognize the body signals of various emotions so they can be mindful of their reactions. It includes a learning guide to help parents engage in meaningful conversations with their children.

What Does It Mean to Be Safe? A Thoughtful Discussion for Readers of All Ages About Drawing Healthy Boundaries and Making Safe Choices by Rana DiOrio, illustrated by Zhen Liu (2019). This book helps kids identify what being safe means: feeling secure and protected and being responsive in any situation. Different settings and contexts for creating safety are covered, including the internet and dealing with bullies or peer pressure.

I Am a Feeling Body: Body Awareness and Mindfulness for Children by Douglas Macauley, illustrated by Ariane Elsammak (2019). This empowering, playful book explores body awareness and mindfulness.

Matt's Swirly World: Helping Parents Raise Mindful Kids, Understand Tantrums and Relieve Stress and Anxiety by Madeleine Matthews, illustrated by Cristina Diana Enache (2019). Shows how emotions can become overwhelming and illustrates positive interactions with parents that teach children to accept these emotions and respond mindfully.

My Body Sends a Signal: Helping Kids Recognize Emotions and Express Feelings by Natalia Maguire, illustrated by Anastasia Zababashkina (2020). In addition to the main story teaching emotional regulation, the book includes calming activities for kids, instructions for adults on follow-up activities, feelings cards, coloring pages, and short stories to teach kids empathy.

When You Are Brave by Pat Zietlow Miller, illustrated by Eliza Wheeler (2019). Encourages children to embrace their inner strength to be brave no matter what they are facing.

Big Bright Feelings series by Tom Percival. This series provides kid-friendly ways to explore common social emotional topics, from being true to yourself to dealing with worries, managing anger, and making friends. Series titles include *Ruby Finds a Worry* (2019), *Perfectly Norman* (2018), *Ravi's Roar* (2020), *Meesha Makes Friends* (2021), and *Tilda Tries Again* (2022).

Visiting Feelings by Lauren Rubenstein, illustrated by Shelly Hehenberger (2013). This book invites readers to become aware of their feelings, and to accept those feelings and ask what they need.

Curiosity, Creativity, and Imagination

The Day the Crayons Quit by Drew Daywalt, illustrated by Oliver Jeffers (2013). A funny book to teach children about creativity, expression, and inclusion.

The Dot by Peter H. Reynolds (2003). Encourages creativity and artistic expression.

What Do You Do with an Idea? by Kobi Yamada, illustrated by Mae Besom (2014). Shows a child nurturing an idea and building the confidence to bring it into the world.

Kindness, Compassion, and Self-Acceptance

Giraffes Can't Dance by Giles Andreae, illustrated by Guy Parker-Rees (2001). Teaches self-acceptance and that each person has unique abilities and talents.

I Am Enough by Grace Byers, illustrated by Keturah A. Bobo (2018). Written by actor and activist Grace Byers, this book teaches children to love who they are, respect others, and be kind to one another.

The Invisible String by Patrice Karst, illustrated by Joanne Lew-Vriethoff (2018). This book presents a simple approach to overcoming separation, loss, and loneliness. The invisible string refers to the bond of care and love that connects us all.

Have You Filled a Bucket Today? A Guide to Daily Happiness for Kids by Carol McCloud, illustrated by David Messing (2015). Encourages positive behavior with the concept of an invisible bucket to show children how easy and rewarding it is to express kindness, appreciation, and love by "filling buckets."

I Am Human: A Book of Empathy by Susan Verde, illustrated by Peter H. Reynolds (2020). Teaches children that we can all make mistakes and that we can all make choices based on compassion and empathy for ourselves and others.

I Am Love: A Book of Compassion by Susan Verde, illustrated by Peter H. Reynolds (2019). Teaches children to live with gratitude, acceptance, and appreciation of others.

Mindfulness Skills and Practice

Here and Now by Julia Denos, illustrated by E. B. Goodale (2019). This book helps kids learn to be in the present moment and to feel connected to and curious about the world around them.

What Does it Mean to be Present? by Rana DiOrio, illustrated by Eliza Wheeler (2010). Children in the book demonstrate the power of being present as they move through different settings (home, school, and the beach).

Mind Bubbles: Exploring Mindfulness with Kids by Heather Krantz, illustrated by Lisa May (2017). This book explains mindfulness in kid-friendly terms. It includes guided mindful breathing scripts for teachers and parents to read so kids can practice new skills.

Wild Mindfulness by Laura Larson, illustrated by Duli Sen (2019). Teaches children to experience mindful moments through guided imagery and breathing techniques as they follow along with a young girl and her adventures camping and exploring in the wild.

The Big Boy with Big, Big Feelings by Britney Winn Lee, illustrated by Jacob Souva (2019). A story of a boy who has waves of overwhelming emotions and how he learns to process them.

Silence by Lemniscates (2012). Using aspects of mindfulness and peaceful meditation, children are asked to pay attention to the world around them.

Moody Cow Meditates by Kerry Lee MacLean (2009). Teaches the basics of meditation to manage strong emotions.

The Lemonade Hurricane: A Story of Mindfulness and Meditation by Licia Morelli, illustrated by Jennifer E. Morris (2015). In this story, one child teaches another how to settle down and be calm and present.

Puppy Mind by Andrew Jordan Nance, illustrated by Jim Durk (2016). In this book, a young boy realizes his mind can be like a puppy, distracted and wandering. He learns to use his breath to focus and tame his puppy mind to be in the present moment.

A Handful of Quiet: Happiness in Four Pebbles by Thich Nhat Hanh (2008). Mindfulness master Thich Nhat Hanh teaches the pebble meditation, a playful activity to introduce children to mindfulness and meditation.

My Magic Breath: Finding Calm Through Mindful Breathing by Nick Ortner and Alison Taylor, illustrated by Michelle Polizzi (2018). In this interactive book, children breathe along as they learn mindfulness, self-awareness, and emotional balance.

Augustus and His Smile by Catherine Rayner (2016). A book to remind children to pause and observe the beauty in the world around them.

Take the Time by Maud Roegiers (2010). Encourages children to slow down and be deliberate with their day-to-day actions and thoughts.

A World of Pausabilities by Frank J. Sileo, illustrated by Jennifer Zivoin (2017). This story is a gentle reminder for kids to stop, take a break, and notice details of the amazing everyday things around them.

Charlotte and the Quiet Place by Deborah Sosin, illustrated by Sarah Woolley (2015). This book teaches mindful breathing and an appreciation for the beauty of silence.

I Am Peace by Susan Verde, illustrated by Peter H. Reynolds (2017). Teaches essential aspects of mindfulness, including listening to and appropriately expressing their emotions, wise decision-making, empathy, and awareness of the present.

Breathing Makes It Better: A Book for Sad Days, Mad Days, Glad Days, and All the Feelings In-Between by Christopher Willard and Wendy O'Leary, illustrated by Alea Marley (2019). Simple guided practices teach children how to apply mindfulness techniques when they need them the most.

Alphabreaths: The ABCs of Mindful Breathing by Christopher Willard and Daniel Rechtschaffen, illustrated by Holly Clifton-Brown (2019). This book teaches mindful breathing and awareness through playful activities using the alphabet.

Yoga and Calming

I Breathe by Susie Brooks, illustrated by Cally Johnson-Isaacs (2019). Children are taught child-friendly yoga poses and breathing techniques designed to help them control their emotions.

Good Morning Yoga: A Pose-by-Pose Wake Up Story by Mariam Gates, illustrated by Sarah Jane Hinder (2016). Pose-by-pose yoga for children to practice in the morning.

Good Night Yoga: A Pose-by-Pose Bedtime Story by Mariam Gates, illustrated by Sarah Jane Hinder (2015). Pose-by-pose yoga to help children relax and prepare for sleep.

Yoga Animals in the Forest: Jump, Stretch, Balance, Breathe, and Relax with the Animals by Christiane Kerr, illustrated by Julia Green (2020). Children are taught yoga poses by all the animals in the forest.

Books for Independent Readers

Be More Yoda: Mindful Thinking from a Galaxy Far Far Away by Christian Blauvelt (2017). Ages 13–17. A book for older Star Wars lovers that uses photos and instructions to teach mindfulness to budding Jedis.

Just Be series by Mallika Chopra, illustrated by Brenna Vaughan. Ages 8–12. Colorful illustrated guides on mindfulness meditation and social-emotional learning. Titles include *Just Breathe* (2018), *Just Feel* (2019), and *Just Be You* (2021).

This Moment Is Your Life (and So Is This One): A Fun and Easy Guide to Mindfulness, Meditation, and Yoga by Mariam Gates, illustrated by Libby VanderPloeg. Grades 5–9. A guide on mindfulness, meditation, and yoga for teens and tweens featuring exercises to build a mindfulness practice.

Master of Mindfulness: How to Be Your Own Superhero in Times of Stress by Laurie Grossman, Angelina Alvarez, and Mr. Musumeci's 5th Grade Class (2019). Ages 5–12. An illustrated guide to building confidence and becoming your own mindfulness superhero for school-age children.

What to Do When You Worry Too Much by Dawn Huebner, illustrated by Bonnie Matthews (2005). Ages 6–12. A workbook to help children cope with anxiety and worry using effective coping strategies and interactive exercises.

What to Do When Your Temper Flares: A Kid's Guide to Overcoming Problems with Anger by Dawn Huebner, illustrated by Bonnie Matthews (2007). Ages 6–12. A workbook to help kids manage anger and strong emotions with effective coping strategies.

Mindfulness for Teen Anger: A Workbook to Overcome Anger & Aggression Using MBSR & DBT Skills by Mark C. Purcell and Jason R. Murphy (2016). A workbook to help teens cope with anger using the proven approaches of mindfulness-based stress reduction and dialectical behavior therapy.

A Kids Book about Mindfulness by Caverly Morgan (2020). Teaches kids how to be present with their thoughts and helps them learn that mindfulness can lead to understanding who they are and why that matters.

Mindful Me: Mindfulness and Meditation for Kids by Whitney Stewart, illustrated by Stacy Peterson. Grades 3–7. An illustrated introduction to mindfulness for kids that features breathing, relaxation, and guided meditation exercises in addition to teaching readers core concepts of mindfulness. Accompanying activity book also available.

The Relaxation and Stress Reduction Workbook for Kids: Help for Children to Cope with Stress, Anxiety, and Transitions (2008) by Lawrence E. Shapiro and Robin K. Sprague. A workbook with guided meditations and activities to help children learn relaxation and coping skills to manage stress.

Apps for Kids on Mindfulness and SEL

BetterSleep. Collection of audio content to help with sleep, including soundscapes, stories, and guided meditations.

Calm. A meditation app for people at all experience levels. Includes a content collection for kids.

Chill Outz. An app with fun stories to promote mindfulness in children and help them relax.

Emotionary. Helps people of all ages identify their primary emotion through visual depictions.

EQ Mighty. Teaches social-emotional intelligence to kids through interactive videos.

Headspace. A meditation app for people at all experience levels that includes a content collection for kids.

Medito. Free app offering guided meditations and more.

Quandary. Learning game that teaches students ethical decision-making and other skills to align with Common Core standards, including social-emotional learning, empathy, and communication, among many others.

Smiling Mind. App from the Australian organization of the same name dedicated to mindfulness and children's mental health. Includes daily meditations and exercises for people of all ages.

Stop, Breathe & Think Kids. A helpful app to help kids pause for brief mindfulness activities and identify their emotions.

SuperBetter. Uses the framework of gameplay to help users make real-life changes and develop positive habits.

Touch and Learn—Emotions. Helps children learn and recognize emotions through pictures. Teachers can use the app to introduce students to new (or existing) concepts regarding emotions and behavior.

Podcasts for Educators
Mindfulness and Compassion Podcasts

Guided Meditations from the Yoga Bunny. A series of guided mindfulness lessons connected with yoga and mind-body practices such as the body scan. theyogabunny.com.

The JOY Factor hosted by Julia Hanson. Each episode focuses on a different topic, many related to mindfulness and well-being. thejoyfactorpodcast.com.

Mindfulness for Beginners hosted by Shaun Donaghy. Mindfulness lessons for beginners focusing on a variety of topics. anchor.fm/shaun-donaghy.

Mindfulness in Eight Weeks hosted by Michael Chaskalson. An eight-week mindfulness training program. mindfulnessworks.com/audio_series/mindfulness-in-eight-weeks-meditations.

Mindful Mama: Parenting with Mindfulness hosted by Hunter Clarke-Fields. Podcast on a variety of topics related to parenting, well-being, and mindfulness. mindfulmamamentor.com/blog/Resources/podcast.

The Mindfulness Meditation Podcast hosted by Danny Ford. A series of guided meditations. mindfulnessandpsychotherapy.com/mindfulness-meditation-podcast.

Mindfulness Meditation Podcast from the Rubin Museum. Unique lessons where guided meditations are inspired by pieces of art. rubinmuseum.org/page/mindfulness-meditation-podcast.

Practicing Human hosted by Cory Muscara. The host discusses the practice and principles of mindfulness and Buddhism, making them accessible to listeners. Each episode covers a topic with a short meditation. practicinghuman.buzzsprout.com.

The Science of Happiness hosted by Dacher Keltner, founder of the Greater Good Science Center at UC Berkeley. The show hosts guest experts in a range of related fields, including mindfulness, SEL, compassion, gratitude, and happiness. greatergood.berkeley.edu/podcasts.

Ten Percent Happier with Dan Harris. Dan Harris, author of *Ten Percent Happier*, presents mindfulness practices and methods for coping with stress in daily life to achieve happiness. tenpercent.com/podcast.

Wake Me Up hosted by Tyler Brown. Podcast to help people wake up in the morning with motivations, routines, and short meditations. wakemeuppodcast.com.

SEL Podcasts

The CharacterStrong Podcast from CharacterStrong. This podcast focuses on character development as a way to help students develop emotional intelligence and social emotional awareness. characterstrong.com/blog/list/tag/Podcast.

Grow Kinder from Committee for Children. Interviews with experts in education, business, technology, and art with the common goal of spreading kindness. cfchildren.org/podcasts.

Move This World with Sara: Conversations in Social-Emotional Learning hosted by Sara Potler LaHayne. Interviews with experts in SEL aimed at building listeners' capacity to implement SEL with practical skills practice in each episode. movethisworld.com/move-this-world-with-sara-sel-podcast.

Neuroscience Meets SEL hosted by Andrea Samadi. Provides tools and resources based on current neuroscience to implement SEL programs in schools and workplaces. andreasamadi.podbean.com.

Our Moral Compass by Dan Wolfe. Daily quotes applied to moral development and one of the five areas of SEL. our-moral-compass.com.

Real Talk for Real Teachers hosted by Becky Bailey. Discusses trends in social emotional learning and classroom management. conscious-discipline.com/e-learning/podcast.

Scholarly Self Care hosted by Tia Barnes. Helps educators, caregivers, and parents improve their SEL and well-being. redcircle.com/shows/scholarly-self-care.

SEL Convergence by Thom Stecher. Discusses child development and SEL from a holistic perspective. anchor.fm/selconvergence.

SELementary hosted by Frameworks of Tampa Bay. Focused on the principles and practice of SEL and ways to implement them into daily life. anchor.fm/frameworkstb.

Teaching Behavior Together hosted by Maria. Provides strategies for teachers to improve classroom management while integrating SEL strategies. teachingbehaviortogether.com/podcast.

Websites, Organizations, Books, and Articles for Educators

Children's Mental Health

WEBSITES AND ORGANIZATIONS

Child Mind Institute

childmind.org

Organization devoted to research and programs related to children's mental health.

Smiling Mind

smilingmind.com.au

Organization promoting mindfulness and children's mental health and well-being.

BOOKS AND ARTICLES

Foxman, Paul. 2004. *The Worried Child: Recognizing Anxiety in Children and Helping Them Heal.* Alameda, CA: Hunter House.
Identifies the causes of worry and anxiety in children and offers ways to support them.

Greene, Ross W. (1998) 2014. *The Explosive Child: A New Approach for Understanding and Parenting Easily Frustrated, Chronically Inflexible Children.* Fifth edition. New York: Harper.
Describes an approach for working through challenges with children who easily become frustrated and dysregulated.

Growth Mindset
BOOKS AND ARTICLES

Canva Team. "The Importance of Fostering Creativity in the Classroom." Medium. medium.com/canva/the-importance-of-fostering-creativity-in-the-classroom-34c94b99281d.
Article identifying the benefits of instilling creativity into classrooms.

Dweck, Carol S. 2007. *Mindset: The New Psychology of Success.* New York: Ballantine.
Book from the researcher who identified the concepts of growth and fixed mindsets.

Duckworth, Sylvia. "12 Benefits of Creativity" infographic. Listed in "My Top 10 Sketch notes in 2016." *Sylvia Duckworth* (blog). sylviaduckworth.com/2016/12/28/top-10-sketchnotes-2016/.
Visual aid showing different benefits of creativity in kids.

Vanlint, Nicola. "The Positive Benefits of Creativity." Life Labs. Kelsey Media, December 14, 2017. lifelabs.psychologies.co.uk/posts/4292-the-positive-benefits-of-creativity.
Article describing the benefits of creativity for children.

Guided Meditations
WEBSITES AND ORGANIZATIONS

A Mindful Edge
amindfuledge.com
Guided meditations and a live weekly meditation you can join via Zoom.

Mindfulness Exercises
mindfulnessexercises.com/free-mindfulness-exercises
A series of guided meditations and discussions related to mindfulness, including a large library of free exercises.

Tara Brach
tarabrach.com
Website of Tara Brach, founder of the Insight Meditation Community of Washington, DC. Site includes hundreds of free guided meditations.

UCLA Mindful Awareness Research Center
uclahealth.org/marc
Guided meditations and lectures from experts.

YogiApproved.com
Website with guided meditations and videos for yoga practice and healthy living.

CLASSROOM SUPPLIES, LESSON PLANS, AND RESOURCES

Fleming, Jessica. "Mindfulness Meditation for Kids—ages 5–17." Udemy. Updated December 2019. udemy.com/course/mindfulness-meditations-for-kids-ages-5-17.
Guided meditations and printable handouts for students.

The Mind-Body Connection
WEBSITES AND ORGANIZATIONS

Yoga Ed.
yogaed.com
Training programs for bringing yoga and mindful movement into schools and youth organizations.

BOOKS AND ARTICLES

Bauer, Susan. 2018. *The Embodied Teen: A Somatic Curriculum for Teaching Body-Mind Awareness, Kinesthetic Intelligence, and Social and Emotional Skills*. Berkeley, CA: North Atlantic Books.

A curriculum based in the mind-body connection to teach teens about body awareness and somatic processing of social-emotional experiences.

Clark, Carrie. "Calming Children: Self Calming Strategies." Speech & Language Kids. speechandlanguagekids.com/calming-children-self-calming-strategies.

Guide for parents and educators to support kids in the practice of calming strategies.

Jewell, Tim, and Crystal Hoshaw. "What Is Diaphragmatic Breathing?" Healthline. Medically reviewed by Courtney Sullivan. Updated November 5, 2021. healthline.com/health/diaphragmatic-breathing.

Article describing the benefits to diaphragmatic breathing with instructions for practicing it.

Kostelyk, Sharla. "Calming Your Child's Fight, Flight or Freeze Response." The Chaos and the Clutter. thechaosandtheclutter.com/archives/helping-child-fight-flight-freeze-mode#.

Article describing the "fight, flight, or freeze" response and how it affects children. Provides specific strategies for children to calm this biological response.

Miller, Caroline. "How to Help Children Calm Down." Child Mind Institute. The Child Mind Institute Family Resource Center. childmind.org/article/how-to-help-children-calm-down.

Article describing different strategies for helping children to calm down when upset or overwhelmed.

Mindfulness in Education
BOOKS AND ARTICLES

Eva, Amy L. 2018. "How to Cultivate Curiosity in Your Classroom." *Greater Good*, September 25, 2018. greatergood.berkeley.edu/article/item/how_to_cultivate_curiosity_in_your_classroom.

Article about ways to integrate curiosity and critical thinking into the classroom.

Jennings, Patricia. 2015. "Seven Ways Mindfulness Can Help Teachers." *Greater Good*, March 30, 2015. greatergood.berkeley.edu/article/item/seven_ways_mindfulness_can_help_teachers.

Ways that mindfulness can improve the well-being and educational environment for teachers.

Marusak, Hilary A. 2021. "How Kids Can Benefit from Mindfulness Training." *The Conversation*. January 5, 2021. theconversation.com/how-kids-can-benefit-from-mindfulness-training-151654.

Discusses ways that mindfulness can improve the learning and emotional health of children.

Olson, Kirke. 2014. *The Invisible Classroom: Relationships, Neuroscience & Mindfulness in School*. New York: W.W. Norton.

Integrates research from brain science and mindfulness to describe how educators can improve social-emotional health and learning environments for students.

CLASSROOM SUPPLIES, LESSON PLANS, AND RESOURCES

Greenland, Susan Kaiser. 2017. *Mindful Games Activity Cards: 55 Fun Ways to Share Mindfulness with Kids and Teens*. With Annaka Harris. Boulder, CO: Shambhala Publications.

Activity cards that teach mindfulness skills to children and teens.

Relax Kids

relaxkids.com

A collection of books, audiobooks, and other products geared to help children become resilient and give them tools and techniques to manage their emotional and mental health.

Stewart, Whitney, and Mina Braun. 2017. *Mindfulness for Kids: 50 Mindfulness Activities for Kindness, Focus and Calm*. Concord, MA: Barefoot Books.

This boxed card deck includes fifty creative mindfulness games, visualizations, and exercises divided into five categories to help children feel grounded, find calm, improve focus, practice loving kindness, and relax.

Mindfulness Skills and Practice

WEBSITES AND ORGANIZATIONS

Mindful

mindful.org

The website for the magazine of the same name. This site has a section for kids, as well as sections on meditating, improving sleep, getting to a calmer state, learning about anxiety, and more.

Mindful Kids

mindfulkidscommunity.org

A website by a team of experts organized to inspire mindfulness in children.

Pocket Mindfulness

pocketmindfulness.com

A father's blog of mindfulness resources, filled with bite-size chunks of useful wisdom and great resources for motivated adults.

BOOKS AND ARTICLES

Brach, Tara. 2020. *Radical Compassion: Learning to Love Yourself and Your World with the Practice of RAIN.* New York: Penguin Life.

Teaches how the RAIN meditation practice can help people overcome negative beliefs and find the courage to live a fuller life during difficult times.

Chödrön, Pema. 2013 *How to Meditate: A Practical Guide to Making Friends with Your Mind.* Louisville, CO: Sounds True.

Renowned American-born Tibetan Buddhist nun Pema Chödrön explores in-depth what she considers the essentials for a lifelong meditation and mindfulness practice.

Collard, Patrizia. 2014. *The Little Book of Mindfulness: 10 Minutes a Day to Less Stress, More Peace.* New York: Hachette.

The author shows how to bring simple five- and ten-minute practices into your day in order to free yourself from stress and find more peace in your life.

Harris, Dan. 2019. *10% Happier: How I Tamed the Voice in My Head, Reduced Stress Without Losing My Edge, and Found Self-Help That Actually Works—A True Story.* New York: Dey Street Books.

TV personality Dan Harris describes his own experiences dealing with anxiety and how mindfulness and meditation helped him to improve his life.

Kabat-Zinn, Jon. 2016. *Mindfulness for Beginners: Reclaiming the Present Moment and Your Life.* Louisville, CO: Sounds True.

Provides the basic practices and principles behind mindfulness-based stress reduction (MBSR).

Nhat Hanh, Thich. 2017. *The Art of Living.* New York: HarperOne.

Mindfulness master Thich Nhat Hanh presents seven transformative meditations that open up new perspectives on our lives, our relationships, and our interconnectedness with the world around us.

Salzberg, Sharon. 2010. *Real Happiness: The Power of Meditation; A 28-Day Program.*

A structured learning program from one of the leaders in mindfulness and meditation, this book covers fundamentals from breathing and posture to calming the mind and larger issues of compassion and awareness.

Stahl, Bob, and Elisha Goldstein. 2019. *A Mindfulness-Based Stress Reduction Workbook.* Oakland, CA: New Harbinger Publications.

A leader in mindfulness guides readers through an interactive workbook teaching the lessons that are part of the mindfulness-based stress reduction (MBSR) eight-week Program.

Neuroscience and Mindfulness

BOOKS & ARTICLES

Boehnke, Kevin, and Richard E. Harris. 2021. "How Two Neuroscientists Built a Mindfulness Class to Improve Students' Well-Being." *Nature* 592 (7855): 645–646. https://doi.org/10.1038/d41586-021-00928-w.

An article describing how teachers used mindfulness and neuroscience to improve the learning environment and social emotional health of graduate students.

Goleman, Daniel, and Richard J. Davidson. 2018. *Altered Traits: Science Reveals How Meditation Changes Your Mind, Brain, and Body.* New York: Avery.

Cutting-edge research from experts Daniel Goleman and Richard Davidson. The authors show what meditation can really do for us by demonstrating the lasting personality traits that mindfulness meditation can create.

Hanson, Rick. 2009. *Buddha's Brain: The Practical Neuroscience of Happiness, Love, and Wisdom*. Oakland, CA: New Harbinger Publications.
Describes the neuroscience behind the well-being produced from mindfulness and meditation.

Hanson, Rick. 2016. *Hardwiring Happiness: The New Brain Science of Contentment, Calm, and Confidence*. New York: Harmony Books.
Lays out a simple method that uses the power of everyday experiences to build new neural structures for happiness and well-being.

Social-Emotional Learning (SEL)
WEBSITES & ORGANIZATIONS
CASEL
casel.org
Research and training in SEL.

Choose Love
chooselovemovement.org
Choose Love offers its Next-Generation Character Social Emotional Development programs to schools nationwide.

The Zones of Regulation
zonesofregulation.com
Training, curriculum, and resources related to the Zones of Regulation SEL Program created by Leah Kuypers.

BOOKS & ARTICLES
Baraz, James, and Michele Lilyanna. 2016. "How to Awaken Joy in Kids." *Greater Good*, October 10, 2016. greatergood.berkeley.edu/article/item/how_to_awaken_joy_in_kids.
This article from the authors of *Awakening Joy for Kids* describes how mindfulness and compassion can instill joy in children.

Erwin, Jonathan C. 2019. *The SEL Solution: Integrate Social and Emotional Learning into Your Curriculum and Build a Caring Climate for All*. Minneapolis: Free Spirit Publishing.
A guide for integrating SEL into classrooms and schools.

Eva, Amy L. 2017. "How to Nurture Empathic Joy in Your Classroom." *Greater Good*, February 2, 2017. greatergood.berkeley.edu/article/item/how_to_nurture_empathic_joy_in_your_classroom.
Describes research on empathic joy shared between teachers and students and its positive impact on learning.

Goleman, Daniel. (1995) 2020. *Emotional Intelligence: Why It Can Matter More than IQ*. 25th Anniversary Edition. New York: Bantam Books.
Identifies and explores several key factors related to emotional intelligence, including self-awareness, self-discipline, and empathy.

Immordino-Yang, Mary Helen. 2016. *Emotions, Learning, and the Brain: Exploring the Educational Implications of Affective Neuroscience*. New York: W.W. Norton & Company.
Mary Helen Immordino-Yang—an affective neuroscientist, human development psychologist, and former public school teacher—presents the neuroscientific connection between emotion and learning.

Mindfulness and SEL Programs and Organizations
Calm Classroom
calmclassroom.com
Provides training and support to educators for implementing mindfulness in schools.

CARE for Teachers
createforeducation.org/care/care-program
Cultivating Awareness and Resilience in Education (CARE) is a professional development program through CREATE for Education. Helps teachers to manage stress and create positive learning environments.

Greater Good Science Center

greatergood.berkeley.edu

Mindfulness and compassion organization based at UC Berkeley and its online magazine.

InsightLA

insightla.org

Los Angeles–based organization providing mindfulness practice workshops, retreats, and community-action programs.

Little Renegades

littlerenegades.com

Materials and resources for creating mindfulness groups and classes in schools.

Mindful Littles

mindfullittles.org

Organization dedicated to integrating mindfulness into families and communities.

Mindful Schools

mindfulschools.org

Offers training and curricula for implementing mindfulness-based programs in schools.

Niroga Institute

niroga.org

Training and teacher education in developing trauma-informed mindfulness programs in schools and organizations.

Peace of Mind

teachpeaceofmind.org

Integrates mindfulness-based SEL, conflict resolution, and social justice into a weekly program for students from pre-K through middle school.

UCLA Mindful Awareness Research Center

uclahealth.org/marc

Mindfulness education and research center. Offers free programs and resources, including the UCLA Mindful app.

UCSD Center for Mindfulness

cih.ucsd.edu/mindfulness

Research, teacher training, and other resources for mindfulness.

REFERENCES

Abrams, Heidi. 2008. "Towards an Understanding of Mindful Practices with Children and Adolescents in Residential Treatment." *Residential Treatment for Children & Youth* 24 (1–2): 93–109. doi.org/10.1080/08865710802147497.

Altmann, Jennifer. 2014. "Power to the People." *Princeton Alumni Weekly*. April 2, 2014. paw.princeton.edu/article/power-people.

Baer, Ruth A., ed. 2014. *Mindfulness-Based Treatment Approaches: Clinician's Guide to Evidence Base and Applications*. Burlington, MA: Academic Press.

Bauer, Clemens C. C., Liron Rozenkrantz, Camila Caballero, Alfonso Nieto-Castanon, Ethan Scherer, Martin R. West, Michael Mrazek, Dawa T. Phillips, John D. E. Gabrieli, and Susan Whitfield-Gabrieli. 2020. "Mindfulness Training Preserves Sustained Attention and Resting State Anticorrelation between Default×Mode Network and Dorsolateral Prefrontal Cortex: A Randomized Controlled Trial." *Human Brain Mapping* 41 (18): 5356–5369. doi.org/10.1002/hbm.25197.

Beauchemin, James, Tiffany L. Hutchins, and Fiona Patterson. 2008. "Mindfulness Meditation May Lessen Anxiety, Promote Social Skills, and Improve Academic Performance among Adolescents with Learning Disabilities." *Complementary Health Practice Review* 13 (1): 34–45. doi.org/10.1177/1533210107311624.

Bernard, Michael E., Ann Vernon, Mark Terjesen, and Robyn Kurasaki. 2013. "Self-Acceptance in the Education and Counseling of Young People." In *The Strength of Self-Acceptance: Theory, Practice and Research*, edited by Michael E. Bernard, 155–192. New York: Springer. doi.org/10.1007/978-1-4614-6806-6_10.

Bertin, Mark. 2015. "Mindfulness Meditation: Guided Practices." *Mindful*, November 9, 2015. mindful.org/mindfulness-meditation-guided-practices/.

Bishop, Scott R., Mark Lau, Shauna Shapiro, Linda Carlson, Nicole D. Anderson, James Carmody, Zindel V. Segal et al. 2004. "Mindfulness: A Proposed Operational Definition." *Clinical Psychology: Science and Practice* 11 (3): 230–241. doi.org/10.1093/clipsy.bph077.

Brach, Tara. 2018. "Reflection: Learning to Stay (4:41 Min.)." Tara Brach (website), September 26, 2018. tarabrach.com/reflection-learning-stay.

Brown, Nathalie. 2013. "How I Teach Children Acceptance." Easy Peasy Kids, July 22, 2013, easypeasykids.com.au/acceptance.

Burnette, Jeni L., Jeffrey M. Pollack, Rachel B. Forsyth, Crystal L. Hoyt, Alexandra D. Babij, Fanice N. Thomas, and Anthony E. Coy. 2019. "A Growth Mindset Intervention: Enhancing Students' Entrepreneurial Self-Efficacy and Career Development." *Entrepreneurship Theory and Practice* 44 (5): 878–908. doi.org/10.1177/1042258719864293.

CASEL (website). n.d. Collaborative for Academic, Social, and Emotional Learning. Accessed November 10, 2021. casel.org.

Centers for Disease Control and Prevention. 2021. "Data and Statistics on Children's Mental Health." Centers for Disease Control and Prevention. US Department of Health and Human Services. Updated March 22, 2021. cdc.gov/childrensmentalhealth/data.html.

Chiesa, Alberto, and Alessandro Serretti. 2009. "Mindfulness-Based Stress Reduction for Stress Management in Healthy People: A Review and Meta-Analysis." *The Journal of Alternative and Complementary Medicine* 15 (5): 593–600.doi.org/10.1089/acm.2008.0495.

Condon, Paul, Gaëlle Desbordes, Willa B. Miller, and David DeSteno. 2013. "Meditation Increases Compassionate Responses to Suffering." *Psychological Science* 24 (10): 2125–2127. doi.org/10.1177/0956797613485603.

ConnectABILITY. n.d. "Calming Strategies to Use with Children." ConnectABILITY. Community Living Toronto. Accessed November 13, 2021. connectability.ca/2010/09/23/calming-strategies-to-use-with-children.

Conversano, Ciro, Alessandro Rotondo, Elena Lensi, Olivia Della Vista, Francesca Arpone, and Mario Antonio Reda. 2010. "Optimism and Its Impact on Mental and Physical Well-Being." *Clinical Practice & Epidemiology in Mental Health* 6 (1): 25–29. doi.org/10.2174/1745017901006010025.

Cunningham, Bob. "The Importance of Positive Self-Esteem for Kids." 2021. Understood. Understood For All Inc., April 14, 2021. understood.org/articles/en/the-importance-of-positive-self-esteem-for-kids.

Durlak, Joseph A., Roger P. Weissberg, Allison B. Dymnicki, Rebecca D. Taylor, and Kriston B. Schellinger. 2011. "The Impact of Enhancing Students' Social and Emotional Learning: A Meta-Analysis of School-Based Universal Interventions." *Child Development* 82 (1): 405–432. doi.org/10.1111/j.1467-8624.2010.01564.x.

Dwan, Evan. "Lessons for Living: Curiosity and Growth Mindset." 2020. Evan Dwan Website, June 26, 2020. evandwan.com/lessons-living-curiosity-growth-mindset.

Engert, Veronika, Bethany E. Kok, Ioannis Papassotiriou, George P. Chrousos, and Tania Singer. 2017. "Specific Reduction in Cortisol Stress Reactivity after Social but Not Attention-Based Mental Training." *Science Advances* 3 (10): 1–13. doi.org/10.31231/osf.io/8d7ez.

Eva, Amy L. 2018. "How to Cultivate Curiosity in Your Classroom." *Greater Good*, September 25, 2018. greatergood.berkeley.edu/article/item/how_to_cultivate_curiosity_in_your_classroom.

Ghandour, Reem M., Laura J. Sherman, Catherine J. Vladutiu, Mir M. Ali, Sean E. Lynch, Rebecca H. Bitsko, and Stephen J. Blumberg. 2019. "Prevalence and Treatment of Depression, Anxiety, and Conduct Problems in US Children." *The Journal of Pediatrics* 206: 256–267. doi.org/10.1016/j.jpeds.2018.09.021.

Goldin, Philippe R., and James J. Gross. 2010. "Effects of Mindfulness-Based Stress Reduction (MBSR) on Emotion Regulation in Social Anxiety Disorder." *Emotion* 10 (1): 83–91. doi.org/10.1037/a0018441.

Greco, Laurie A., and Steven C. Hayes. 2008. *Acceptance & Mindfulness Treatments for Children & Adolescents: A Practitioner's Guide.* Oakland, CA: New Harbinger Publications.

Jha, Amism P., Jason Krompinger, and Michael J. Baime. 2007. "Mindfulness Training Modifies Subsystems of Attention." *Cognitive, Affective, & Behavioral Neuroscience* 7 (2): 109–119. doi.org/10.3758/cabn.7.2.109.

Kabat-Zinn, Jon. (1994) 2014. *Wherever You Go, There You Are: Mindfulness Meditation in Everyday Life.* New York: Hachette.

Kelly, Kate. 2020. "The Importance of Mindfulness for Kids Who Learn and Think Differently." Understood. Understood For All Inc., October 20, 2020, understood.org/articles/en/mindfulness-kids-who-learn-think-differently.

Krisbergh, Audrey. n.d. "Kids and Courage." The Center for Parenting Education. Accessed November 13, 2021. centerforparentingeducation.org/library-of-articles/self-esteem/kids-and-courage.

Kram, Gabriel Ethan. 2011. *Applied Mindfulness: Inner Life Skills for Youth.* Edited by James Daren Dickinson. Self-published, CreateSpace.

Kvam, Siri, Catrine Lykkedrang Kleppe, Inger Hilde Nordhus, and Anders Hovland. 2016. "Exercise as a Treatment for Depression: A Meta-Analysis." *Journal of Affective Disorders* 202: 67–86. doi.org/10.1016/j.jad.2016.03.063.

Layous, Kristin, S. Katherine Nelson, Eva Oberle, Kimberly A. Schonert-Reichl, and Sonja Lyubomirsky. 2012. "Kindness Counts: Prompting Prosocial Behavior in Preadolescents Boosts Peer Acceptance and Well-Being." *PLOS ONE* 7 (12). doi.org/10.1371/journal.pone.0051380.

Lee, Jennifer, Randye J. Semple, Dinelia Rosa, and Lisa Miller. 2008. "Mindfulness-Based Cognitive Therapy for Children: Results of a Pilot Study." *Journal of Cognitive Psychotherapy* 22 (1): 15–28. doi.org/10.1891/0889.8391.22.1.15.

Leonard, Nancy H., and Michael Harvey. 2007. "The Trait of Curiosity as a Predictor of Emotional Intelligence." *Journal of Applied Social Psychology* 37 (7): 1914–1929. doi.org/10.1111/j.1559-1816.2007.00243.x.

KidsHealth. "Your Child's Self-Esteem (for Parents)." 2018. Nemours KidsHealth. The Nemours Foundation. Updated July 2018. kidshealth.org/en/parents/self-esteem.html.

Männikkö, Niko, Heidi Ruotsalainen, Jouko Miettunen, Halley M. Pontes, and Maria Kääriäinen. 2020. "Problematic Gaming Behaviour and Health-Related Outcomes: A Systematic Review and Meta-Analysis." *Journal of Health Psychology* 25 (1): 67–81. doi.org/10.1177/1359105317740414.

Marine Corps Community Services. n.d. "7 Reasons Why Teaching Children Kindness Is Essential." Marine Corps Community Services. US Marine Corps. Accessed November 13, 2021. usmc-mccs.org/articles/7-reasons-why-teaching-children-kindness-is-essential.

Mendelson, Tamar, Mark T. Greenberg, Jacinda K. Dariotis, Laura Feagans Gould, Brittany L. Rhoades, and Philip J. Leaf. 2010. "Feasibility and Preliminary Outcomes of a School-Based Mindfulness Intervention for Urban Youth." *Journal of Abnormal Child Psychology* 38 (7): 985–994. doi.org/10.1007/s10802-010-9418-x.

Mightier. 2021. "What Is the 'Mind-Body Connection?'" Mightier. Neuromotion Labs, June 12, 2021. mightier.com/articles/what-is-the-mind-body-connection/.

Napoli, Maria, Paul Rock Krech, and Lynn C. Holley. 2005. "Mindfulness Training for Elementary School Students." *Journal of Applied School Psychology* 21 (1): 99–125. doi.org/10.1300/j370v21n01_05.

Netz, Yael. 2017. "Is the Comparison between Exercise and Pharmacologic Treatment of Depression in the Clinical Practice Guideline of the American College of Physicians Evidence-Based?" *Frontiers in Pharmacology* 8: 257. doi.org/10.3389/fphar.2017.00257.

Oberle, Eva, Kimberly A. Schonert-Reichl, Molly Stewart Lawlor, and Kimberly C. Thomson. 2012. "Mindfulness and Inhibitory Control in Early Adolescence." *The Journal of Early Adolescence* 32 (4): 565–588. doi.org/10.1177/0272431611403741.

Open Circle Mindfulness. 2017. "The RAIN Formula, Meditative Investigation, and Calming Emotions." Open Circle Mindfulness, January 23, 2017. opencirclemindfulness.org/the-rain-formula-and-meditative-investigation.

Ortner, Catherine N. M., Sachne J. Kilner, Philip David Zelazo. 2007. "Mindfulness Meditation and Reduced Emotional Interference on a Cognitive Task." *Motivation and Emotion* 31 (4): 271–283. doi.org/10.1007/s11031-007-9076-7.

Price-Mitchell, Marilyn. 2015. "Curiosity: The Force within a Hungry Mind." Edutopia. George Lucas Educational Foundation, February 17, 2015. edutopia.org/blog/8-pathways-curiosity-hungry-mind-marilyn-price-mitchell.

Racine, Nicole, Brae Anne McArthur, Jessica E. Cooke, Rachel Eirich, Jenny Zhu, and Sheri Madigan. 2021. "Global Prevalence of Depressive and Anxiety Symptoms in Children and Adolescents during COVID-19." *JAMA Pediatrics* 175 (11): 1142–1150. doi.org/10.1001/jamapediatrics.2021.2482.

Roemer, Lizabeth, Sarah Krill Williston, and Laura Grace Rollins. 2015. "Mindfulness and Emotion Regulation." *Current Opinion in Psychology* 3: 52–57. doi.org/10.1016/j.copsyc.2015.02.006.

Semple, Randye J., and Jennifer Lee. 2011. *Mindfulness-Based Cognitive Therapy for Anxious Children: A Manual for Treating Childhood Anxiety.* Oakland, CA: New Harbinger Publications.

Semple, Randye J, Elizabeth F. G. Reid, and Lisa Miller. 2005. "Treating Anxiety with Mindfulness: An Open Trial of Mindfulness Training for Anxious Children." *Journal of Cognitive Psychotherapy* 19 (4): 379–392. doi.org/10.1891/jcop.2005.19.4.379.

Sileo, Frank. 2020. "The Power of the Pause: Helping Your Child Learn about Mindfulness in This Stressful Time." Magination Press Family. American Psychological Association, April 2, 2020. maginationpressfamily.org/mindfulness-kids-teens/the-power-of-the-pause-helping-your-child-learn-about-mindfulness-in-this-stressful-time.

Singh, Nirbhay N., and Subhashni D. Joy. 2020. "Mindfulness-Based Interventions with Children and Adolescents." In *Mindfulness-Based Interventions with Children and Adolescents: Research and Practice*, edited by Nirbhay N. Singh and Subhashni D. Singh Joy, 3–10. New York: Routledge. doi.org/10.4324/9781315563862-2.

Singh, Nirbhay N., Giulio E. Lancioni, Alan S. W. Winton, Angela D. Adkins, Judy Singh, and Ashvind N. Singh. 2007. "Mindfulness Training Assists Individuals with Moderate Mental Retardation to Maintain Their Community Placements." *Behavior Modification* 31 (6): 800–814. doi.org/10.1177/0145445507300925.

Tartakovsky, Margarita. 2016. "5 Tips for Teaching Your Kids Self-Compassion." Psych Central. Healthline Media, October 6, 2016. psychcentral.com/blog/5-tips-for-teaching-your-kids-self-compassion.

Thompson, Miles, and Jeremy Gauntlett-Gilbert. 2008. "Mindfulness with Children and Adolescents: Effective Clinical Application." *Clinical Child Psychology and Psychiatry* 13 (3): 395–407. doi.org/10.1177/1359104508090603.

Vanlint, Nicola. 2019. "The Positive Benefits of Creativity." Life Labs. Kelsey Media, February 16, 2019. lifelabs.psychologies.co.uk/posts/4292-the-positive-benefits-of-creativity.

Vipassana Hawai'i. n.d. "R.A.I.N. ~ D.R.O.P." vipassanahawaii.org/resources/raindrop.

von Stumm, Sophie, Benedikt Hell, and Tomas Chamorro-Premuzic. 2011. "The Hungry Mind: Intellectual Curiosity Is the Third Pillar of Acdemic Performance." *Perspectives on Psychological Science* 6 (6): 574–588. doi.org/10.1177/1745691611421204.

Welch, Chad. 2020. "How to Help Children Calm Down." Door County Partnership for Children and Families. Door County Parents, April 9, 2020. doorcountyparents.com/how-to-help-children-calm-down.

INDEX

To download the reproducible forms and other digital content for this book, visit **freespirit.com/pcc-forms**. Use the password **2connect**.

ABOUT THE AUTHORS

Mark Purcell, Psy.D., (drmarkpurcell.com) is a clinical psychologist who specializes in treating children and families with emotional regulation challenges. He has been working in various aspects of the mental health field for over twenty years. Mark's professional experience has ranged from providing psychotherapy to children to developing specialized treatment programs and teaching professionals and graduate students. In addition to teaching and training, he provides therapy in his private practice. Mark has particular interests in mindfulness-based therapeutic approaches, such as DBT and MBSR. He also has research interests in the effects of trauma and effective treatment modalities. He coauthored *Mindfulness for Teen Anger*, which integrates these interests into a self-help workbook for adolescents. He lives and works in the San Francisco Bay Area. Follow him on Twitter @dr_mark_purcell.

Kellen Glinder, M.D., is a pediatrician and site lead for the Silicon Valley office of Private Medical. He is also the emeritus chair of pediatrics at the Palo Alto Division of the Palo Alto Medical Foundation and an adjunct clinical assistant professor at Stanford University. He is active in both the American Academy of Pediatrics and the American Academy of Allergy, Asthma, and Immunology. As a Wilderness Medical Society member, he enjoys figuring out how to get kids outside often and with smiles. Kellen is a Screen Actors Guild member, has trained as an improvisational actor, and has taught classes in medical improv and the art of communication, including a course at the Dartmouth Geisel School of Medicine. He lives in the heart of Silicon Valley, California. Follow him on Twitter @drglinder.